EXPLORE
GUERNSEY
ALDERNEY, HERM AND SARK

TIM EARL

With photographs by Brian Green

LOCAL HERITAGE BOOKS

EXPLORE GUERNSEY
Alderney, Herm and Sark
by Tim Earl

First Published 1985
© Tim Earl 1985

LOCAL HERITAGE BOOKS
3 Catherine Road, Newbury,
Berkshire
and 36 Queens Road, Newbury,
Berkshire

Series Editor: John Woodward
Typesetting and Artwork: Publicity Plus, Newbury
Sketch maps by Roy Skyrme
Produced through
MRM (Print Consultants) Ltd, Reading, Berkshire
Printed in Guernsey by The Guernsey Press Co.

ISBN 0 86368 012 7

BIBLIOGRAPHY

David Bellamy, *Coastal Walks; Grassland Walks*

C.E.B. Brett, *The Buildings in the Town and Parish of St Peter Port*

Alan Barber, *Walks with a Car in Guernsey*

Bob Burns, *A Field Guide to the Archaeological Sites of Guernsey*

Victor Coysh, *Alderney; Afoot in Alderney*

G. Stevens Cox, *A Pictorial History of Guernsey*

J. Stevens Cox, *Prehistoric Monuments of Guernsey*

Tim Earl, *A Field Guide to the Birds of Guernsey*

Marie De Garis, *Dictiounnaire Angllais — Guernesiais; Folklore of Guernsey*

Gareth Griffin, *Shore Fishing Around Guernsey*

Ken Hawkes, *Sark*

Ian Kinnes, *Les Fouaillages and Megalithic Monuments of Guernsey*

L. James Marr, *Guernsey People*

Winston G. Ramsey, *The War in the Channel Islands; Then and Now*

Jenny Page and Patience Ryan, *A Field Guide to the Wild Flowers of Guernsey*

Patrick A. Wootton, *The Story of Lihou Island*

Back copies of *The Guernsey Evening Press*
Transactions of La Societe Guernesiaise

ACKNOWLEDGEMENTS

To my wife Marilyn, to whom this book is dedicated, and who helped and encouraged me throughout its preparation, heart-felt thanks.
Nick Le Messurier for reading the manuscript.
Derek Poole, the finest tour bus driver in Guernsey.
The States of Guernsey Philatelic Bureau for permission to use illustrations of stamps.
Bill Tipping for his picture of a loose-flowered orchid.
To the following who read some sections of the manuscript: George Bramall, Rona Cole, Heather Sebire, Ken Tough, Jenny Page and Tim Peet.

FOREWORD

by Sir Charles Frossard,
Bailiff of Guernsey.

With more than 53,000 people living on an island such as Guernsey, the history of which goes back nearly 8,000 years, it must surprise no one that there is a wide range of pastimes, enterprises and places to visit, where great things have happened and still do. There are books and publications to cover all interests, from natural sciences, the island's language, its history and government, to guides on a wide range of the Guernseyman's daily activities.

But what if you are not a specialist, if your interest is in many things, and like most of us your time is short? *Explore Guernsey* will undoubtedly prove to be an important guide, not only for the annual visitor, but also for many of us who live on the island. The book leads the reader around Guernsey, parish by parish, pointing out the interesting features and prompting further study.

It is appropriate that two trained observers have been recruited to be our eyes and ears on the journey - both Tim Earl and Brian Green work for the *Guernsey Evening Press* and are thus embroiled in the minutiae of island life. *Explore Guernsey* has fulfilled a long-felt need for a work to bring all aspects of island life together in a convenient and eminently readable volume.

CONTENTS

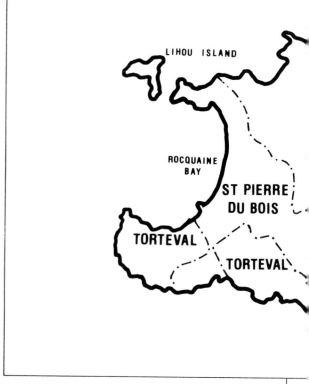

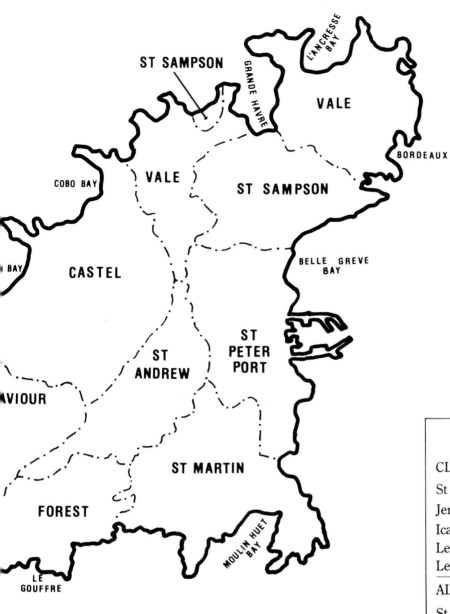

INTRODUCTION

Guernsey cattle

I t is customary to start a book of this kind with a quick look at the geology and geography of the place to be explored. But a short career in journalism has persuaded me that the most important feature of the world we live in is people.

V ery little of this book does not involve the effect that successive generations of Guernseymen and women had on the island.

A rchaeologists tell us that the first mesolithic (middle Stone Age) settlers were eating ormers, a local shellfish delicacy, as they sat around furze fires on the sandy plains of L'Ancresse Common between seven and eight thousand years ago. These were primitive men, but their society was so well organised that they could employ vast teams of people to move the huge stones which today can be found all over the Common. Their activities may have continued for thousands of years, becoming better organised and using more refined techniques as they took up stone carving, built bigger tombs and shifted granite pieces weighing more than ten tons.

O ur neolithic (late Stone Age) forefathers marked the passing of their chieftains with tombs at Les Vardes, Dehus and Le Creux es Faies. They erected the standing stones at La Longue Rocque and Fort Le Crocq, put up the astounding Gran' Mere du Chimquiere where St Martin's Church was to be founded, and colonised Herm and Alderney.

St Sampson's Harbour

E vidence of Bronze Age activity is scarce, but a tumulus was built at the Hougue Fouque and a promontory fort was established at Jerbourg. Arrowheads and pottery have been found at that site and along the cliff paths of the south coast.

I ron Age Guernseymen continued to fortify Jerbourg Point while in Alderney an impressive settlement and pottery has been discovered at Les Huguettes. A small double-banked hillfort, destined to become the Vale Castle, was established north of the Braye du Valle, now St Sampson's Harbour. Some late Iron Age settlers were wealthy and privileged warriors, buried with their swords, knives, spears, pottery and personal ornaments in graves along the west coast. A small settlement found in St Peter Port suggests that even around the time of Christ there was a trading route between northern France and southern England which used Guernsey as a staging post.

R omans certainly made use of the Green Island, as they called Guernsey, and evidence from wrecks found off St Peter Port and a settlement in the town back this up. Amphorae from southern Spain have been found, and coins seem to have been dropped by careless soldiers in all the islands. The Nunnery on Longis Common in Alderney has a strange herringbone design in its walls and Roman artifacts have been found in the area around it; there is a theory that this was one of a chain of shore forts put up by the Romans to combat the growing menace of pirates who robbed their ships.

Alderney Harbour

Traditional crabpot making

T he early saints visited the island between A.D. 500 and A.D. 850 - St Sampson is said to have been the first. There were few people to hear his sermons in those days, but an oratory was set up where he landed in the north of Guernsey. It was later to be the site of St Sampson's Church.

K ing John of England lost Normandy in 1204 but retained possession of the Channel Islands, fortifying them heavily with a chain of castles which in Guernsey included Castle Cornet, and the Chateau des Marais to the north of St Peter Port. The people of Guernsey suddenly found themselves under English rule, no longer part of Normandy. They were given their own charters by King John and today's government and legal system began to evolve.

I n 1643, the English Civil War embroiled the islands and, occupied by lieutenant-governor Sir Peter Osborne, Castle Cornet was to become the last Royalist stronghold in Britain to surrender to the parliamentary forces. The Governor and his troops held out for nearly nine years, during which time he bombarded the citizens of St Peter Port, who supported Cromwell, using cannon which were supposed to be defending the channel between Guernsey and Herm. The Governor was supplied from Jersey, which was also loyal to the Crown. The bitterness engendered by the Civil War caused a rift between Guernsey and Jersey which, although it has now healed, still shows itself in the great rivalry between the islands.

Trading, smuggling and privateering became the order of the day during the 17th and 18th centuries and some Guernsey people became very wealthy. Trouble with France in the late 18th century encouraged frenzied military activity, and army engineers gave the island much of its present appearance by draining the Braye du Valle, forging military roads across the island and building a series of forts to defend the coast.

The harbour of St Peter Port was enlarged to accommodate the trading boom stimulated by the feeling of safety brought on by the new defences. Steam packets plied between Guernsey and England towards the end of the last century, and the first tourists must have arrived on those ships. More than 220,000 now come to the island each year.

Expansion of the tourist industry was blocked by visitors of another sort when the island was occupied by the Germans during the Second World War. many of the school children, my mother and two uncles among them, were evacuated to the UK before the troops arrived. They were cut off from their families for nearly five years, and it is difficult to work out who had the worst of the arrangement. It must be remembered that those left behind could not know about the liberation which was to come on 9 May 1945.

Far Right: St Peter Port Harbour

Right: Herm Boat

Below: At Alderney Harbour

8

The Germans used slave labour, from the occupied countries of eastern Europe, to build their fortifications around the island. Few shots were fired against the allies, and historians argue that the Channel Islands contributed indirectly to the allied war effort because the materials and German troops were deployed to no effect when they could have been elsewhere.

The Germans also occupied Alderney, Sark and Herm - the area known as the Bailiwick of Guernsey. This gets its name because it is governed by a Bailiff, who is appointed by the Crown. The area includes the islands of Brecqhou and Jethou which are in private hands.

The parliament of the Bailiwick is the States of Deliberation, referred to throughout the islands as the States. The assembly is made up of 12 conseillers, senior politicians elected by their peers, 33 deputies, for whom the island votes in general elections, 10 parish representatives and two members from Alderney. The Bailiff presides over the House as civil head of the island. Parishes are governed by 12 elected people called a douzaine.

Left: Sausmarez Manor Railway   Below: Herm Prison

Above: Castle Cornet Gardens

9

Above: St Peter Port

The States set local taxation, issue Guernsey's stamps and money, and administer the internal affairs of the island such as health, education, roads, housing, and the local industries. In foreign affairs, the UK departments responsible act on behalf of the States. The formalities and voting carried out in the House are still performed in French although the debates are in English.

The principle industry providing employment is horticulture, although the tourist industry has now grown so large that the two compete for that distinction. Banking is probably the biggest revenue-earner for the States, and increasing numbers of young people are being trained for jobs in the finance industry. A considerable section of St Peter Port has been taken over by banks and names reflecting the cosmopolitan nature of the industry can be seen.

Guernesiais, the local Norman-French language, is still spoken in some of the more remote parts of the island, although it is dying out and everyone can now speak English. It is responsible for the sing-song lilt in which English is spoken and, of course, many of the place names came into use when Guernesiais was the sole language.

Right: Swallowtail Butterfly

The oldest postbox in Britain: Union Street, St Peter Port

F rench place names are one of the reasons many people get lost on the island. Contrary to popular belief, getting lost is not a problem restricted to visitors — many locals get lost too but rarely own up! Lanes and roads are like coins, they have two different appearances, depending which side you look at. However hard you try to memorise a route it looks different on the way back. Some parishes try to improve matters by putting signs on the road junctions, but people still get lost. Fortunately this often turns into a pleasurable diversion, and it is certainly a good way to explore Guernsey.

T he island's roads and lanes were not designed for the motor car, which is better left at home. People who choose to explore on foot will certainly see the best in each island. The countryside is criss-crossed by little lanes which wind and turn, run up hills and down into valleys, providing variety with every step taken. The wildlife is a mixture of British and mainland European, and many Mediterranean plant, insect, bird and reptile species have been recorded. Migrating birds stop in the spring and autumn and during cold winters large numbers seek Guernsey's frost-free shores.

G ardens reflect the mild climate, with a wide range of plants, normally kept in green-houses, growing outside. Fuchsia plants in the Fermain and Petit Bot valleys grow to a height of 30ft and in autumn the Guernsey lily, *Nerine sarniensis,* can be seen flowering in gardens all over the island.

P erhaps the best places for flowers are the cliff walks in spring. May and June see the 16-mile walk from St Peter Port to Pleinmont looking like a huge rock garden. The same applies to cliff walks in Herm and Sark, though Alderney holds the crown for its natural unspoilt beauty. People even refer to it as the Cinderella of the Channel Islands — like her it has two ugly sisters, they say.

G uernsey and Jersey cannot be described as ugly, but they are different from each other as well as from Alderney. Much of the difference comes from the cliffs and the way the islands slope as a result. Jersey looks like a piece of France pulled into the sea - her cliffs are in the north and the productive farmland thus faces south and grows potatoes and vegetables for the early English markets.

G uernsey slopes away from her south coast cliffs and so faces north, giving a slightly cooler climate. The crops are grown under glass and have to be watered and looked after several times each day, so the dwellings have been built close to the greenhouses and ribbon development has spread across the countryside.

B ut what development — no two houses are the same, all have little characteristics which make them of interest. Witches' seats placed close to chimney stacks so that the old crones have no excuse to enter the house; marriage stones over the front doors making the union between families; ancient carved stones which have been incorporated into the masonry - all add to the character of Guernsey buildings.

T he best feature of Guernsey is the one I started this introduction with — people, Sarnians as we 'Guerns' are called, who still have time to talk, to inquire about who you are, who your ancestors were or where you are staying. It is a charming curiosity which prompts the question, which is not reserved for visitors, but aimed at anyone exploring Guernsey.

Above: Alderney Harbour
Right: St Peter Port model
yacht pond
Below left:
La Seignurie, Sark
Below right: The Arcade,
St Peter Port

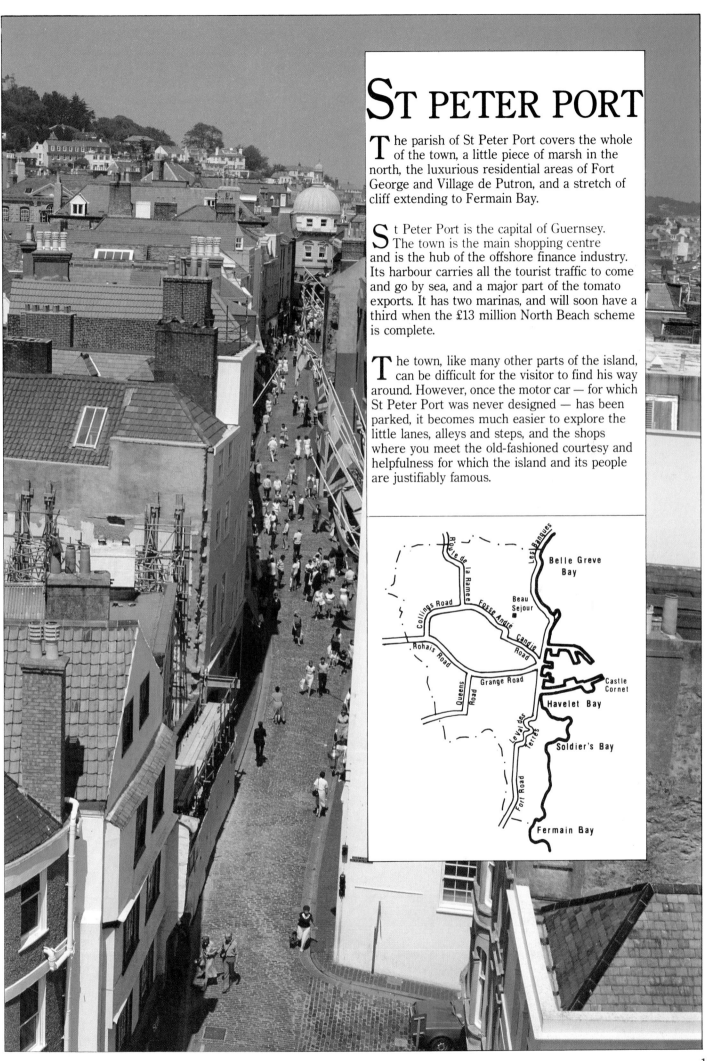

ST PETER PORT

The parish of St Peter Port covers the whole of the town, a little piece of marsh in the north, the luxurious residential areas of Fort George and Village de Putron, and a stretch of cliff extending to Fermain Bay.

St Peter Port is the capital of Guernsey. The town is the main shopping centre and is the hub of the offshore finance industry. Its harbour carries all the tourist traffic to come and go by sea, and a major part of the tomato exports. It has two marinas, and will soon have a third when the £13 million North Beach scheme is complete.

The town, like many other parts of the island, can be difficult for the visitor to find his way around. However, once the motor car — for which St Peter Port was never designed — has been parked, it becomes much easier to explore the little lanes, alleys and steps, and the shops where you meet the old-fashioned courtesy and helpfulness for which the island and its people are justifiably famous.

THE ROYAL COURT HOUSE

Perry's map ref: town plan F6

This beautiful building is the meeting place of the island's parliament - The States of Deliberation - and houses the offices of the Bailiff, who presides over both the States and the Royal Court. Island archives, going back continuously for more than 400 years, are kept in the Greffe, or record room, on the ground floor of the Royal Court House. These include registers of property deeds, births, marriages and deaths, together with files on all companies incorporated in Guernsey.

The Royal Court, which with its various divisions corresponds with the County, Crown and High Courts of England and Wales, and the Magistrate's Court both sit in the Royal Court House. Records of their proceedings and the official tape recordings of States debates are also kept in the Greffe.

The building overlooks St Peter Port and is to be found to the south of the War Memorial at the top of Smith Street. It was built between 1799 and 1802 and was altered to the designs of John Wilson in 1822. To mark the Diamond Jubilee of Queen Victoria the court house was greatly improved and the Magistrate's Court and present Greffe Office added between 1900 and 1902. The Royal Court chamber was renovated in 1948-9. The most recent addition, when a third court room — La Cour Ordinaire — was opened to house the civil divisions of the Royal Court, was in 1982.

There are two public entrances to the building. The main entrance is at the top of a stone flight of steps and leads into a paved entrance hall with the Greffe door on the right. Wilson's geometric staircase leads up from this foyer to the Royal Court chamber and La Cour Ordinaire. The staircase walls are lined with boards detailing donations to the four charities administered by the Royal Court, the earliest legacy dating from 1588.

Inside the Royal Court chamber

The decor of Royal Court chamber is impressive with the pre-1837 version of the royal coat of arms, incorporating the arms of Hanover, above the Bailiff's chair. There is a large public gallery reached by turning left at the top of the main staircase. Royal Court sittings, before the Bailiff and jurats, take place every Thursday morning, and on other days if a trial is being heard or there is a great deal of work to be done. The Bailiff, or his deputy, and the jurats preside over the court dressed in their ceremonial robes with French-style hats — wigs have never been worn in Guernsey courts.

On the last Wednesday of each month, except August, the States of Deliberation meet in the Royal Court chamber. The Bailiff again presides and, as in the Royal Court, the clerk is HM Greffier, who sits at a table in front of the Bailiff, facing the members of the house.

The Bailiff is accompanied on the bench by 12 conseillers - the island's senior politicians, elected by the House. In the main part of the chamber, the majority of places are taken by the 33 elected deputies, but at the side of the room, towards the rear, sit 10 douzaine representatives, one from each parish, and two representatives from Alderney.

Proceedings start with the Lord's Prayer, said in French by the Greffier, and a roll call of the members present. The first, and often most interesting part of the meeting proper is question time, when the presidents of committees have to face queries on their policies from members of the House. This is followed by an agenda set out in a publication called the Billet d'Etat. Each item may be discussed or go through without debate, depending on the wishes of members.

The public gallery is rarely full, which is surprising when one considers that the States meetings set the stamp on life in Guernsey. Taxation and how the money is to be spent, social conditions and international relations, speed limits and who does what in boats off the island's shores, decisions affecting tourism, growing, finance and retail business are all decided by the House.

At least half the members are elected by the people of Guernsey and their performance in the debates can be fascinating. There are no political parties on the island and the public has to vote for individuals — whose views often vary considerably along with their ability to get them over. The show is well worth watching.

THE TOWN CHURCH

This church is considered the most beautiful in the Channel Islands and is often referred to as St Peter Port Cathedral. It reflects the wealth of an earlier community whose trading activities gave the solid financial base upon which the island's present stability rests. The church was built on the instructions of William the Conqueror, 16 years before his epic Battle of Hastings victory, and it has given successive rectors pleasure to think that the Te Deum may have echoed around the building in celebration of the event!

It stands a little way back from the southern corner of the Victoria Marina, the port's old harbour, and at one time was surrounded by houses - the last was demolished in 1914. The main entrance to the building is through the north porch in Church Square.

The nave is reached by walking past two rows of pews; turn left to face the altar and your back is to the west door. A few paces foward takes you to the crossing, the site of the original humble church built on the foreshore of what was then a fishing village. It had very thick walls, for the church served not only as a place of worship but also as a refuge when the village was attacked by pirates. This original small church was enlarged by adding buildings to either side and piercing the connecting walls with pointed arches to give the spacious area we have today. The west door with its rounded Norman arch is still in place.

The south transept was added in 1466, the date on a beam now hidden by plaster, and makes use of more delicate, slender pillars than the huge Norman piers which support the central tower above the crossing. The chancel, leading to the altar, is screened by a wrought iron lattice and houses the choir stalls. These were carved by Harry Hems of Exeter and installed in 1886. They depict scenes from the life of St Peter, the church's patron saint.

Most of the windows were blown out during the last war when the Americans bombed a German submarine believed to be in St Peter Port harbour, and one bomb exploded on the quay. The replacement window over the altar is known as the liberation window, and has scenes based on the hymn of praise, Te Deum.

The monuments in the church are numerous and of great interest as they chronicle the history of Guernsey's major families. They include memorials to General Sir Isaac Brock, who was called 'the man who saved Canada' after his British troops beat the Americans at the Battle of Queenston Heights, Canada on 13 October 1812. It was the end of a distinguished military career for Brock, who was killed in the battle. There is also a memorial to Peter Perchard, a Lord Mayor of London who died in 1806. Not all the monuments are to conventionally great men; the modest tablet to Captain Nicholas Le Messurier records that he was captain of a privateer, killed while attempting to capture a French Indiaman in February 1759!

BUDGET LIVES UP TO ITS NAME IN HOLIDAY RENTALS

New Cars each year Fitted Radios in all Cars		Economy Mini City	Group A New Ford Fiesta BL Metro VW Polo	Group B B.L. Metro Auto. Ford Escort Saloons/Estates V.W. Golf B.L. Maestro	Group C Ford Sierra Saloons & Estates
Low Season Jan. 1st to May 17th Oct. 1st to Dec. 31st	Daily	£3.45	£3.95	£4.75	£5.45
	Weekly	£23.00	£27.50	£33.00	£38.00
	Per day after 7 days	£3.20	£3.80	£4.50	£5.25
Mid Season May 18th to July 12th Sept. 7th to Sept. 30th	Daily	£4.75	£5.45	£6.25	£6.95
	Weekly	£33.00	£38.00	£43.00	£48.00
	Per day after 7 days	£4.50	£5.25	£6.00	£6.75
High Season July 13th to Sept. 6th	Daily	£6.25	£6.95	£7.75	£9.95
	Weekly	£43.00	£48.00	£54.00	£69.00
	Per day after 7 days	£6.00	£6.75	£7.50	£9.75

FREE!

OF CHARGE

. . . EXTRA DRIVERS . . . DELIVERY AND COLLECTION
. . . PARKING DISCS . . . RADIOS IN ALL CARS
. . . MAPS . . . MOTORING INFORMATION
NO V.A.T.
7 DAY 24 HOUR PERSONAL SERVICE

FORT ROAD MOTORS LTD.

P.O. BOX 180,
FORT ROAD,
ST. PETER PORT,
GUERNSEY.
TEL. 0481 38706/21930

AIRPORT DESK,
LA VILLIAZE,
FOREST.
TEL. 0481 37670

P.O. BOX 180,
LES CAMPS,
ST. MARTIN'S
GUERNSEY.
TEL. 0481 36632

Budget
rent a car

Price. Our unfair advantage.

THE MARKETS

The Vegetable Market

Perry's map ref:
town plan G7

Markets seem to have a fascination for everyone — even the modern hypermarkets in the French ports seem to attract a far larger following than their duty-free status might warrant. The Guernsey markets, found in a large triangular complex of buildings just above the Town Church, have a very special appeal.

Until the mid eighteenth century, street markets were held from Berthelot Street, down High Street to Cow Lane - the little alley that runs from Church Square to the harbour — and around three sides of the Town Church. They eventually became unpopular as the smell of fish, slaughtered meat, and rotting vegetables, noise of the assembly and packs of vermin attracted by the offal did not go down well with the rather well-to-do worshippers in the Church. The fruit market even used to shelter in the church during bad weather!

Eventually, the covered market, on the right as you come up the steps into Market Square, was built between 1780 and 1782 to house the street vendors. Originally used by butchers, its function was changed after the present Meat Market was built on the other side of the square in 1822. The covered market was then named the French Halles as the produce sold was shipped from Brittany.

Above the French Halles are the Old Assembly Rooms, also opened in 1782 and preached in by John Wesley five years later. They were built by a select society of gentlemen and were used to hold dances or assemblies. These were for natives only, with the exception of officers of the garrison, and although boots were allowed to be worn, spurs were not!

Higher up Market Street, above the French Halles, is the building which used to house the 'Queen's weights'. A sales tax was levied on all market goods which were weighed on balances known as the Queen's or King's scales. The weights and measures are now in Candie Museum, and their original home, built in 1876, has been converted into a restaurant.

The French Halles were soon too small for the market traders who supplied the growing community of St Peter Port. In 1821 architect John Wilson was invited by the States to solve the problem for ever and build an enclosed meat market. The New Market was opened over the road from the French Halles the following year.

Seven years later the next section - Les Arcades — was opened to provide accommodation for a fish market. Later in the century, when again facilities proved insufficient, a new architect, John Newton, was taken on to complete the complex. The new Fish Market with its remarkable roof was followed by the Lower Vegetable Market (completed by Francis Chambers) towards the end of the century.

Turn left at the bottom of the stairs leading to the aerial arcade and walk into the Meat Market. As well as the permanent butchers' stalls, you will find a wide range of both British and European produce on sale. Sausages from Germany and Belgium, a great deal of French produce, including long loaves flown to the island daily, and cheeses from Switzerland and Italy, all combine to give the market a wonderful aroma.

The special thing about all the markets is that the smell of one is left behind as you wander into the next. With no mechanical ventilation aids, the building is so designed that the natural draughts take the smells upwards and away — a feat most modern markets cannot achieve even with extractor fans!

This is important as the next area you enter is the Fish Market. Here is a sight for anglers' sore eyes — the stalls are laden with the most beautiful specimen fish. Much of the produce is locally caught, although some has to be imported during the months that the small local fishing fleet cannot cope with demand. Besides the wet fish there is also a good selection of crabs, lobsters and crayfish.

Your entrance into the Fish Market was close to the apex of the triangular building, the fish stalls lying along the second side, parallel to Fountain Street. This arm continues down into the Fruit and Vegetable Market with its mixture of French and English produce. Many of the local vegetables are marked with their patois names and indeed the market is one of the few places outside the country areas in which you can expect to hear the local language spoken.

At the end of this market, a short flight of stairs leads down into the Flower Market in the very short base of the triangular building.

Here one of the island's main exports is on display. Guernsey flowers are renowned for their quality and variety. Gerberas in delicate shades of apricot, lemon and pink, exotic Bird of Paradise flowers, new varieties of chrysanthemum and scented freesias are all on show in season.

Above the tiers of flowers, on top of the capitals of the supporting columns, the floral theme of the Flower Market is continued in stone. Turn left at the bottom of the steps into the market and a short walk will return you to the Market Square.

CASTLE CORNET

Perry's map ref: p. 25 H1
Open: daily, summer only,
10.00 - 5.00
Price guide B
Parking: model yacht pond,
Castle Esplanade

Because of the protection it afforded to the main shipping routes to Bordeaux and Bayonne by its position on an island overlooking the roadsteads, Castle Cornet is partly responsible for the success of St Peter Port during the last 800 years. Although armaments used over that time have developed out of all recognition, the strategic importance of the site has not changed — as shown by the reinforcements added to the building during the German Occupation.

Besides offering a fascinating historical excursion, the castle enjoys some of the finest views of the island, and an interesting time can be spent watching ships come and go, just as all the sentries have done since 1206, when the first records of munitions and materials for the castle were documented.

Castle Cornet is now joined to St Peter Port by a raised stone pier which forms the southern arm of the harbour. A bridge connects this to the fort and the Castle Walk, a jetty leading to the lighthouse.

The 16th-century entrance, tucked back-to-front in the seaward side of the town bastion to protect it from gunfire from the main island, opens under a portcullis into the outer ward. The entrance is overlooked by the saluting battery with an impressive row of black cannon facing the harbour pool.

A flight of steps leads up from the outer ward through a curtain wall to an inner wall, the barbican, which was enlarged by the French during their occupation around 1338. They were pinned down in the castle by attacks from 'Les Anglais' outside and were forced to build new walls from stone picked up or chipped off the islet on which they were isolated. For this reason the French walls are easy to identify as they are made up of very small pieces of stone. The barbican can be seen from St Peter Port, and in medieval times a cage hung from the wall was used to hold prisoners. Their death from starvation and exposure was intended as a warning to other criminals. A lime pit underneath eventually took the bodies.

The entrance to the barbican is guarded by a portcullis. Pass under it onto a path which leads to the site of the second line of defence, a pit and drawbridge. Both are long gone, the pit filled and the drawbridge removed, but under a tower across the path the recess and groove for the mechanism can be seen. A timber supporting the tower dates from 1378.

When the old town gaol was housed in the castle, convicts would be exercised in the barbican, which is why the path is called prisoner's walk. It leads through another 13th-century archway with portcullis into an area where there was once a huge tower and a number of dwellings — the home of the Governor of Guernsey in the 17th century, Lord Hatton, and his family and entourage.

Waiting to fire the noonday gun

The tower was very high and dominated the castle, but in 1672, while it was being used as a gunpowder store, it was struck by lightning during a violent thunderstorm. It blew up, demolishing the houses and killing seven people. The Governor survived but his mother, the Dowager Lady Hatton, and his wife were killed. Guernsey's governors have lived on the main island ever since.

A flight of steps lead up to the citadel on the top of the rocky islet.

Guns trained on St Peter Port Harbour

The route you have followed so far is that which would have been taken by an invading army trying to capture the castle. This would have been a difficult task, probably costing hundreds of lives, and explains the long periods of occupation after the castle did change hands. It took three days of hard fighting to eject the French in 1345, and that was after a siege of seven years!

Another siege, lasting eight and a half years between 1643 and 1651, occurred during the Civil War. Guernsey declared for Parliament but the army in the castle, led by the Governor, Sir Peter Osborne, supported King Charles. During the ensuing occupation more than 10,000 cannonballs were fired into St Peter Port, often on Sunday morning as people were going to the Town Church. Young lads would fight over the cannonballs, and the victor would row out to the castle with the spoils and sell them to the Governor to be used again!

The castle was supplied from the sea by Royalist supporters from Jersey — a fact which is quoted today as a cause of the rivalry between the two islands. This support was in part responsible for Castle Cornet's distinction of being the last stronghold in Britain to give up the Royalist struggle. Sir George de Carteret, the Jerseyman responsible for supplying the castle and defending his native island, was given land in North America for his pains — he named it New Jersey.

Foreign occupation of the castle again took place in the last war and at the citadel you can explore a German machine-gun nest. To assist in range-finding, the outlines of several landmarks which can be seen from the site have been painted on the walls. The Brehon Tower, half way to Herm, is shown as 3,800 metres while Jethou is outlined and given the distance of 5,900 metres.

Further defences are visible as you descend from the summit. A narrow gateway leads to the outer ward. This is called the sally port because defending soldiers could 'sally forth'. If they were followed as they popped back, spears would be thrust through holes in the walls and molten lead poured down a hole above the attackers' heads. The sally port leads into the well battery which stands next to the only well in the fort, although underground cisterns were used to collect rainwater that fell on the building.

Arms on display within the castle

Within the ramparts

The well battery is at one end of a walkway running around the castle between the outer bailey and the 50ft buttressed, medieval inner wall surrounding the citadel. It passes two ammunition magazines, the tops of which are built from rather incongruous Portland stone brought to Guernsey as ships' ballast.

Just beyond the second magazine is the south battery, with its 19th-century mount for a revolving gun, and a shallow flight of steps which leads up to a crenellated wall facing the bathing pools and Havelet Bay. From here, the infantry would fire on attackers, retreating down the steps to reload their guns.

Several other buildings around the courtyard were for the garrison. These include a stores building and the 17th-century sutlers' house behind the hospital up a flight of steps. This was where the sutler — army quartermaster — lived. Today the stores building is used as a museum, as is the top floor of the hospital.

The dominant feature of this area, however, is the medieval Gunners' tower which had a curtain wall running down to the barbican. In 1745 a retaining wall was built above the outer ward, and the curtain wall was demolished. The 20ft-deep hole thus created behind the retaining wall was filled with hardcore to make the courtyard on which the buildings were erected.

From here the path runs down to cross your incoming steps as you go out on to the east or Royal battery, site of the noon-day gun. Daily, a colourful ceremony takes place in which a uniformed man watches the Town Church clock through a telescope while another, on the order 'Fire', sets off the gun. In days gone by the gun was loaded with a loaf of bread and seagulls would plummet through the cloud of smoke catching the pieces. However, one day a joker substituted a large pebble for the bread. This shot into the pool and hit a fishing boat below the water line, sinking it — and the tradition was dropped!

ST PETER PORT HARBOUR

This single feature of the Bailiwick of Guernsey has held the key to the prosperity of the islands from Roman times to the present day. It is fitting that it should give its name to the capital town and the most important parish. The reasons for the success of Guernsey revolve around this harbour and are just as valid today as they were in any other period of its history.

The site has been used as a haven for seafarers since the first boats passed that way. It is sheltered from the prevailing westerly and southerly winds by the island itself, while Herm and Sark ensure that the effect of an easterly blow is minimised. The French mainland of the Bay of St Malo up to Cherbourg Peninsular gives further protection from that quarter.

By the time of William the Conqueror, who as Duke of Normandy was the island's ruler, the village was strategically important and big enough for him to order the building of a church which doubled as a fort against pirates. Two hundred years later, the foundations of a harbour were laid, and a castle built to defend it on an islet off the port.

The harbour started life as a jetty, all remains of which are long gone. There was a simple timber quay by the 13th century, and by 1580 the south jetty had been built using huge boulders piled 35ft high. To the north a pier was added between 1703 and 1750. This created the Old Harbour, now the Victoria Marina, lined on the landward side by old warehouses which have been converted into shops and offices along the sea front.

The larger main harbour was built in successive schemes between 1835 and 1909 incorporating Castle Cornet, which dominates the south breakwater leading into the port. Since then the New Jetty with its passenger terminal and the wall of the Albert Marina have been added.

As this book was being written work on the North Beach marina was in full swing with huge lorries coming to and fro with tons of granite destined for this latest extension to the harbour. The project will leave St Peter Port with a huge car and yacht park on the northern side of the harbour wall.

St Peter Port is a place to watch the coming and going of ships carrying the materials vital to the island and many of the people who visit it. Since 1964, hydrofoils have sped up to its entrance, their skis finally sinking gracefully into the water to obey the six knot speed limit.

Fishing boats — Guernsey has a fleet of about 20 — leave for distant marks, their diesel motors chugging. Container ships with their hidden cargoes come and go while the passenger ferries pour 97,000 excited holidaymakers into the town each year. More than 80,000 trays of tomatoes leave each week of the summer in the holds of coasters or roll-on, roll-off ferries.

The best place to start your exploration is the White Rock, the site of a seabird colony stained white by droppings until the northern harbour arm was built over it. The end of this arm was marked by the tiny cylindrical granite lighthouse built in 1868, but the Germans extended the harbour wall with a bunker, on top of which sits the Signal Station. This is an airport-styled control room from which local shipping movement is co-ordinated.

The dock below this end of the harbour is known as No 6 Berth and is where all the passengers and freight bound for Sark depart. It is best to observe the activity from a distance as the place is dangerous. It can be viewed safely from the walkway above the Sark berth. This leads past the container berth where cargoes from Weymouth, Portsmouth, London and Rotterdam are unloaded.

Further down the walkway is the New Jetty at the end of which is the car ferry terminal with its flat observation roof. All the UK and continental passengers arrive here and the coming and going can be watched easily from the roof. Car ferries dock on the seaward side of the jetty, hydrofoils from St Malo and Jersey at the end. Other passenger craft and the fishing fleet tie up on the landward side.

The New Jetty is built on piles driven into the harbour bed. They have walkways linking them. Several flights of steps leading beneath the jetty take you to another world. The hustle and bustle of the passenger terminal is left behind and wildlife abounds. Occasionally the groynes are used by Kingfishers as the water beneath the jetty often teems with small fish.

Between the jetty and town is the Cambridge Berth on which are the warehouses and cranes which service ships to Alderney. The States Board of Administration offices are also to be found here, enjoying one of the best views of any building in St Peter Port. Passengers from Herm are landed on the Cambridge Berth if the tide is too low for the Trident ferries to reach their booking offices further down the quay. At the junction of the Cambridge Berth and the footpath you have come down is a plaque above the walkway, commemorating the deaths of Guernseymen who were killed by a bombing raid a few days before the Occupation began.

The lifeboat *Sir William Arnold* and the St John Ambulance boat *Flying Christine* are moored in the pool between the Cambridge berth and the New Jetty. Both boats are on permanent alert, the lifeboat for any sea disaster within a 50-mile radius of the harbour, and *Flying Christine* to take ambulance cases from Herm, Sark and passing ships for treatment in St Peter Port. She is sometimes used in cliff rescues — part of her equipment is for firing ropes — carried out by St John Ambulance crews who are trained in the techniques. Their bravery on the cliffs in the area matches that of the lifeboat crews.

The end of the northern arm of St Julian's Pier is marked by a small building with a clock tower, erected in 1891 to house a weighbridge, now made reduntant by containerisation. Turn left here and walk along the pavement towards the Tourist Information Office — a flat building with a green copper roof and welcoming flags. Half way to it, a gate in the wall takes you through to a raised footpath on the other side of the wall. The area it overlooks is the Careening Hard where boats were beached and turned on their sides (careened) so that their hulls could be cleaned or made water-tight. Its seaward side is protected by an arm of the Victoria Pier.

The Old Harbour is now a bustling marina; it is sometimes difficult to see water, so densely-packed are the visiting yachts and motorboats. The mouth of the marina has been dammed to ensure that the boats do not touch bottom even at low tide. As the tide comes in, quite an overfall occurs at the bar of the harbour and a popular sport among local youngsters is to row their dinghies against the current, shooting the rapids on the way back.

The Fermain boats and some of the Herm ferries set off from Albert Pier. Their departure point in the marina is overlooked by a statue of Prince Albert cast in 1863 by Joseph Durham. It looks most odd, as the prince is dressed in the robes of the Order of the Bath — making him look as if he is off to a fancy-dress party. At low tide the ferries leave from the end of the pier, behind the Buccaneer pub.

Opposite the Bus Station beyond the Albert Memorial is the second of the port's marinas. Used by local boats, the Albert Marina was made in 1974 by building a concrete jetty from the Castle Emplacement towards the Albert Pier. Like the Victoria, the Albert Marina has a bar across the mouth to prevent boats from beaching.

The walk down the Castle Emplacement, along the conveniently raised footpath, provides good views of the harbour already explored. The Cambridge Berth and New Jetty stand out, allowing their activities to be watched from afar. The footpath high above the road leads past several granite buildings — the abattoir with its double roof for ventilation, a boat-building firm, and the Guernsey Fishermen's Co-operative. A huge bunker was built further down the Emplacement during the German Occupation.

Towards the end of the Emplacement the jetty widens out. The area is cluttered with beached boats in the winter and cars during the summer, so that the open area created by the Model Yacht Pond is a welcome sight. Opened in 1887, it has been destroyed and rebuilt twice since — in the First World War for use as a French seaplane base and during the Occupation as a vehicle park. On the left of the pond is a chandlery and boat-building firm where most private craft fuel for their next journey. The Guernsey Yacht Club building overlooks the area at the eastern end, next to a cafe housed in a wooden cabin, which is popular with local fishermen.

A short bridge connects the Emplacement to Castle Cornet and the Castle Walk, a long concrete breakwater which leads to the beautiful granite lighthouse designed by Peter Le Lievre and dated 1866. The view from the end, either of the town or across to Herm, Jethou and Sark, is well worth the walk. In winter, a southerly gale combined with high tides produces the most spectacular sea watching imaginable as waves shoot high into the air when they meet the breakwater. It is, of course, impossible to walk beyond the castle in these conditions.

J&S

Established in 1884

The Jewellers & Silversmiths pledges it's future to continue the ties of love and friendship that has been present in their first hundred years.

With three floors of workshops, and qualified gemmologists, and technical staff to advise you, you are assured of the very highest quality products, supported by an excellent service.

Please call in and seek our advice.

Fashionable Gold

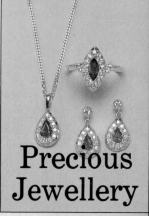

Precious Jewellery

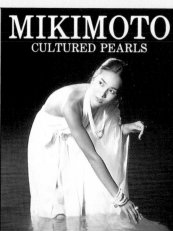

MIKIMOTO
CULTURED PEARLS

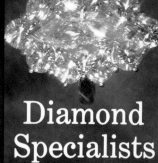

Diamond Specialists

ALBANY
A FLAIR FOR ORIGINALITY IN BONE CHINE & BRONZE

THE GUERNSEY LILY

specially commissioned for our Centenary fine boned chine hand painted thimble £6.00

OMEGA Ω

ROLEX

A traditional jewellery and watch shop, which sells quality goods at affordable prices with a lifetime of experience under the umbrella of the Jewellers & Silversmiths Co.

GWH

The Jewellers & Silversmiths Co. Ltd.
High Street St. Peter Port telephone 23621

22

ST PETER PORT STEPS

Hillsides have always presented town planners with problems, the solution of which often results in something visually appealing. This is certainly the case with St Peter Port's steps, which have been built to connect the distinct levels on which the town is built.

St Barnabas and town steps

North Pier Steps, running from Boots Chemist shop in High Street to the Victoria Marina, are intriguing. As you stand under that arch at the top, two prongs branch off halfway down the main flight of steps, producing the shape of a trident pointing to the sea. Was this a reminder to the Jack Tars walking down the steps of the perils facing them when they joined their ships? The steps were probably built about 1750, as the surrounding area was developed, to serve the north quay of the old harbour. They have echoed to the footsteps of sailors and nautical folk ever since.

That was not the purpose of the three flights leading from the market and Arcade area up to the Regency 'New Town' on the hill above old St Peter Port. These were for servants who worked in the wealthy merchants' houses built above the old town. They would struggle up the the steps with food, cleaning materials and perhaps even fuel bought in the bustling shopping areas below.

Collectively they are known as the Escaliers du Mont Gibel, and individually as the Arcade, Constitution and Clifton Steps. The first climbs up from the side of Maison Carre in the Arcade to Clifton. These were built up a sheer cliff and were dog-legged, with landings to ease the climb. The view from them over the tops of the houses and shops is spectacular. The roofs below are covered with slates and terracotta pantiles, and are dotted with white

and grey dormers. There are few reminders of the present and it is easy to imagine that you are in the 17th century — watch out for little boys popping out of the chimneys with brushes in their hands!

Constitution Steps also come out of Clifton, at the side of the Salvation Army Hall. They branch off Clifton steps which wind up from half way along Market Street, opposite a side entrance to the Meat Market. The flight passes the burnt-out shell of the Little Theatre which was gutted by fire in 1983, and now awaits redevelopment.

THE AQUARIUM

Perry's map ref: p.25 H3 Open: summer 10.00 - 5.00
Price guide B

A disused tunnel designed to connect two popular bays during the last century has now been converted into an aquarium. The tunnel was built during the heyday of granite quarrying, when the skills needed were readily available, to give access through Les Terres Point to Soldiers Bay where people went to swim. During the Occupation it was fortified by the Germans. Something of a folly, the far end came out through a dangerous cliff which is subject to rockfalls. One such in recent times has revealed the exit from the tunnel, which can be seen well through binoculars from the Pepper Pot monument above Fermain Bay.

The aquarium has both tropical and cold-water fish which are displayed in large tanks built into the sides of the tunnel. Sea and freshwater fish are included, with a small number of amphibians and reptiles.

Perhaps the most interesting tanks hold the sea fish which have been caught around Guernsey. These include small shoals of mullet and bass, plaice, turbot and brill, and the highlight, a 6ft-long porbeagle shark. Water for the marine tanks is constantly changed by pumping it from the beach facing the entrance.

A large shallow pond in the aquarium contains several big conger eels. In 1983, this was the site of an unusual selection test for Operation Raleigh, a round-the-world expedition for adventurous youngsters. The would-be participants had to wade into the conger pool and totally submerge themselves among the writhing leviathans — they deserved their trip!

BUCKTROUT & CO. LTD.

Established in 1830, Bucktrouts combine the finest range of
vintage wines at excellent prices with expert advice.
Fondée en 1830, la Maison Bucktrout vous offre la gamme le mieux de
vins de haut qualité aux prix très interessants avec une conseille experte.
Waterloo House, High Street, St. Peter Port.

Guernsey's leading Wine and Spirits
Merchant right on the Quayside
of the Marina.

Le marchand de vins et de spirits le plus
important a Guernsey situe le long
du quai de la marina.

BUREAU DE CHANGE

...plus loads more!

gp GUERNSEY PRESS STATIONERS
8, SMITH STREET, ST. PETER PORT, TEL: 24829

24

VICTOR HUGO'S HAUTEVILLE HOUSE

Perry's map ref: town plan F10

Open: 10.00 - 12.00; 2.00 - 4.30

Price guide B

Parking: in Hautville Road

The 54-year-old novelist, poet and amateur carpenter started his interior decorating in 1856, after buying the house with the proceeds of a volume of poetry written just after his arrival on the island. The house was chosen for the view from his study, past Herm and Sark to the coast of his beloved France.

Besides 'home improvements' Hugo occupied himself writing, walking the beautiful cliff paths and visiting his mistress Juliette Drouet. Their liaison, begun in 1833, only ended with her death in 1883 — she sent Hugo two love letters daily for 50 years! She was installed in a house just up the road from that of her lover, who would rise at six in the morning, have a cold bath on the roof of his house and stand contemplating her window.

The guides who take parties on the 45-minute tour are experts on the house and its former owner, giving detailed commentaries and answering questions with equal authority. From them you will learn that the dining table is reconstructed from antique wardrobes, the panelling around the walls is made from old sideboards tattooed with poker-work, and one of the pelmets is made from two chairbacks, placed upside-down. The dining room walls are covered with blue Delft tiles, and over the mantlepiece huge letter H's are topped by a statue of the Madonna.

The dining room

Hauteville House is owned by the City of Paris, and preserved as a monument to the most famous — and eccentric — writer ever to set foot in Guernsey.

Victor-Marie Hugo was a French poet, novelist and dramatist who led the romantic movement in his native country. He played an active part in politics, serving firstly as a peer under King Louis Philippe before transferring his loyalty to the republicans in 1848. Deeply disturbed by the restoration of the Second Empire under the right-wing Prince Louis-Napoleon, Hugo fled France in 1851 to spend 18 years in the Channel Islands. Hauteville House, in Guernsey, was his home from 1856 to 1870 when he returned to France after the fall of the Second Empire.

He had a great love of liberty, but his hopes for mankind were considered by most to be a pipe dream. What he failed to do politically, Victor Hugo made up for with his writings, and his influence on French literature in the nineteenth century was unrivalled. His best known works for English readers are *The Toilers of the Sea*, which was dedicated to the sailors of Guernsey, *The Hunchback of Notre Dame, Les Miserables, The Man Who Laughed* and *Han of Iceland*.

The evidence of Hugo's eccentricity is to be seen all over his house, which is filled from basement to study attic with the most extraordinary wall coverings, furniture, light fittings and tapestries. Hugo spent much of his time in Guernsey collecting and adapting to his own taste every carved table, chair, four-poster bed and wooden chest he could lay his hands on. The pieces were dissected, sliced into bits, or had their limbs amputated, and were then reassembled in almost unbelievable designs as wall panelling, furniture and objects d'art.

A settee in the tapestry room is covered with carpets while embroidered drapes festoon the walls. The mantlepiece is made from sliced medieval and Renaissance furniture, including some antique bed legs. It is a monument to the poet's heroes, such as Shakespeare, Homer and Moses, whose names are carved on wooden scrolls.

Upstairs on the first floor there are two drawing rooms, one red, the other blue. The red room is sumptuously panelled in red damask and illuminated by chandeliers. Four life-size gilt carved slave figures hold lamps aloft as they stand before an ornate fireplace, in the front of which is embedded the belt of Victor Hugo's Hungarian friend, Colonel Sandor Telki. In the smaller blue room, which opens into a sun lounge, a golden Buddha sits between two huge Chinese vases. The furniture in both rooms is upholstered in silk, and the rooms are lined with mirrors to increase their apparent size.

Victor Hugo returned to France in 1870, but revisited Guernsey in 1872-3 and for a last time in 1878. He died in 1885, two years after his companion Juliette, and was given a state funeral in Paris.

ST JAMES THE LESS

Perry's map ref: town plan G6

Almost demolished to make way for a car park, and nearly made into a police station, this fine old Regency church has now been converted into a concert hall and assembly room. It is well suited to this purpose as it will seat 600 people and has the finest acoustics of any building in the island.

The church was originally built to commemorate the British victory at Waterloo in 1815. The idea was first mooted by Admiral Sir James Sausmarez in October of that year, and by August 1818 St James the Less had been designed, built and consecrated. The architect was John Wilson, and it is said to be his best work.

At a time when most of the islanders spoke Guernesiaise, the services at St James were held in English for the benefit of the British garrison on the island. The church marked one of the boundaries of the "new town" which was springing up on the higher ground above the medieval areas of St Peter Port.

St James the Less is built from local granite with dressed stone window surrounds. The outer walls are plastered in Roman cement and stucco but the northern face is in rough dressed granite. It has a false porch with high artificial fluted Doric columns and huge panelled entrance

St James the Less in 1843

doors. The drum-shaped steeple rises from a square base, past a balcony, to a dome, ball and weathercock more than 110ft above the ground. This spire, which is floodlit at night, is one of the best-known landmarks of St Peter Port, visible from the sea and many parts of the town.

Inside the building there is a horse-shoe shaped wooden balcony which provides an intimate atmosphere for the performers who see the audience around and above them. This balcony is carried by fluted columns which add to the classical feel of the hall. Two cantilevered stone staircases with wrought iron rails lead up to the balcony, and to a delightful circular meeting room above the foyer.

The conversion from church to concert hall was paid for by the States of Guernsey at a cost of £458,000. The building is leased and run by the Friends of St James Association, who aim to attract classical, popular, folk and jazz concerts within its walls. New orchestras and bands are encouraged to use the hall, as are young musicians from local schools. Clubs with varied interests from all over the island meet at the hall and exhibitions are held there occasionally. All the activities are outlined in a leaflet published by the Friends of St James at regular intervals.

GUERNSEY MUSEUM AND ART GALLERY

Candie Gardens

Perry's map ref: town plan E5
Open: 10.30 - 5.30
Price guide B
Parking: Cambridge Park

'The story of the island and its people' was the brief given to architects, builders and the curator of Guernsey Museum when the idea to build it was approved by the States in 1972. In 1979, during its first year, it won the New Museum of the Year Award. The award was well won for besides fulfilling its brief, Candie Museum, as it soon became known, is typical of Guernsey — compact, comprehensive, fascinating thoughout and very good value.

It is built on the site of an old glass and iron concert pavilion, the bandstand of which has been converted into a tea room. The decision to build the museum was taken after St Barnabas, the original home of Guernsey's antiquities, became unsafe and was closed to the public in 1971.

Much of the collection housed at Candie Museum was built up by two men.

Frederick Corbin Lukis started collecting artifacts when he was 23, after being given a skull dug out of La Varde long barrow by militia soldiers in the summer of 1811. His interest fired, he went on to start the Lukis collection. Later, with his four sons, he was responsible for the identification and preservation of many island monuments, a large number of which he excavated.

In later life he wrote up his findings in a series of volumes called *Collectanea Antiqua*, illustrated by his daughter Mary Anne. In 1907 the collection was bequeathed to the States who also bought the family home, Lukis House in the Grange, St Peter Port.

Wilfred Carey's collection of pictures, prints and ceramics was bequeathed in 1929 and eventually housed in St Barnabas, known then as the Lukis and Island Museum. Both collections were added to during the 30 years St Barnabas was open, and they are the basis of the material now on display in Candie.

The museum is organised into a series of eight-sided rooms which link to form the display area, art gallery and a tiny theatre. A flavour of Guernsey is given every hour with a 13-minute film of the island in the theatre. From here, the visitor is encouraged to wander through the display area.

This lays out the history of Guernsey, starting with its geology. The climate and natural history (including mouthwatering specimens of edible chancre crabs, lobsters and crayfish!) are examined and beautiful displays recreate scenes of early island life from neolithic man onwards. The story of the island's defence is told and the museum takes a detailed look at the history of fishing and agriculture on the island.

Many local artifacts are on display, such as the old corn weights — large pebbles, the weight of which has been chipped on the side. The island's official bronze measures, large bucket-like vessels used for measuring the volume of grain, are also on show.

The art gallery was designed with movable screens and your visit to the museum is likely to coincide with a temporary exhibition, such as a display of local artists' work or paintings of the island. The gallery has adjustable lighting and is fully climate-controlled — this is important as most of the pieces on display are water colours.

Local artists Paul Jacob Naftel and his younger contemporary brother Peter Le Lievre, whose work dates from the mid 19th century, have provided a fascinating picture of life in the island during the reign of Queen Victoria. Marine artist Thomas Whitcombe is represented by a painting of shipping off Castle Cornet in 1796.

The museum sits in extensive and beautiful gardens which were left to the people of Guernsey by Osmond Priaulx in 1887. The States spent £300 on exotic plants and the gardens have been a joy for all ever since. A statue of Victor Hugo, designed by J. Boucher in 1914, gazes out to sea below the museum, while keeping him company, higher up the hill, is a statue of Queen Victoria. It was unveiled in 1900, rather late for her Jubilee in 1897, and cost £800.

BEAU SEJOUR LEISURE CENTRE

Perry's map ref: town plan
E2 & E3
Bus route G

More than four million people have visited Beau Sejour since it was opened in December 1976 — vindication of the vigorous campaign to persuade States members that it was a worthwhile investment. The centre is made up of swimming facilities, a theatre, a multi-purpose hall which provides for activities ranging from roller-skating to banqueting, and a sports hall that can also be used for exhibitions and concerts. The complex also functions as an international conference centre.

The designers of Beau Sejour wanted each area of the centre to have a number of functions so that islanders and visitors would be able to choose from a range of activities.

As you enter the centre, the changing rooms for sport and swimming are on the right, and the theatre and bowls hall to the left. Up a flight of stairs in front are meeting rooms, bars, a cafe and viewing gallery for some of the activities.

The swimming pool is heated, cleaned by an osmosis system, and has carpeted surrounds. It is designed for leisure uses, including water polo, synchronised swimming, life saving and canoeing. The pool has no diving stages but can accommodate six 25-metre lanes. Visitors to the health suite's sauna and solarium can cool of with a plunge, and there is a warmer, shallow pool for children.

The Sir John Loveridge Hall is used for a wide range of sporting activities including badminton, basketball, cricket, trampolining, five-a-side football, volleyball and table tennis. Weight training and martial arts sessions are carried out in rooms opening on to the hall. Squash is played in five courts next to the large hall.

Occasionally everything is cleared from the 15,200 sq. ft hall to make way for exhibitions (Ideal Home, flowers and boating are popular), concerts seating up to 1,800 people, a dance festival or conference. During the summer occasional shows, and even circus performances, are staged.

Some of the trade exhibitions and larger conferences have spilled over into the Sarnia Hall. Normally used for roller-skating, the hall has extensive kitchens attached and can seat 600 people for a dinner. A few local firms are large enough to hold their staff functions in the hall and occasionally the big spenders among conferences arrange for the culinary talent in local hotels to roll out the red carpet for their delegates. At such times you are likely to see huge butter sculptures and the most exotic dishes gracing the tables.

Between the Sarnia Hall and theatre is an intimate bar in the Green Room. Here fans of the local repertory group discuss their latest offering, film buffs debate the performances of the stars, and the merits of visiting lecturers are evaluated by whichever audience has just spilled out for the interval.

Such excitement is not expressed by the draughts, scrabble or bridge players who do battle in any one of several smaller rooms upstairs. Nor does it reach the frenzied heights of youngsters dancing to records in The Dungeon.

Keep-fit class

Outside in summer, younger children thrill to the speed of the astroglide — a huge slide — or bounce around on the inflated Koncord Kastle while their elders play tennis. There is a fine bowls green which is popular with both locals and visitors to Guernsey. In winter the sports pitches are used for football and hockey.

Conference delegates have their own entrance and reception area at the back of the centre. This is a recent addition and provides a luxurious introduction to the place that may be home for the next few days. It connects directly to the Sir John Loveridge and Sarnia Halls, linking the two, and is sometimes used for trade stands during very large exhibitions.

An exhibition in the Sir John Loveridge Hall

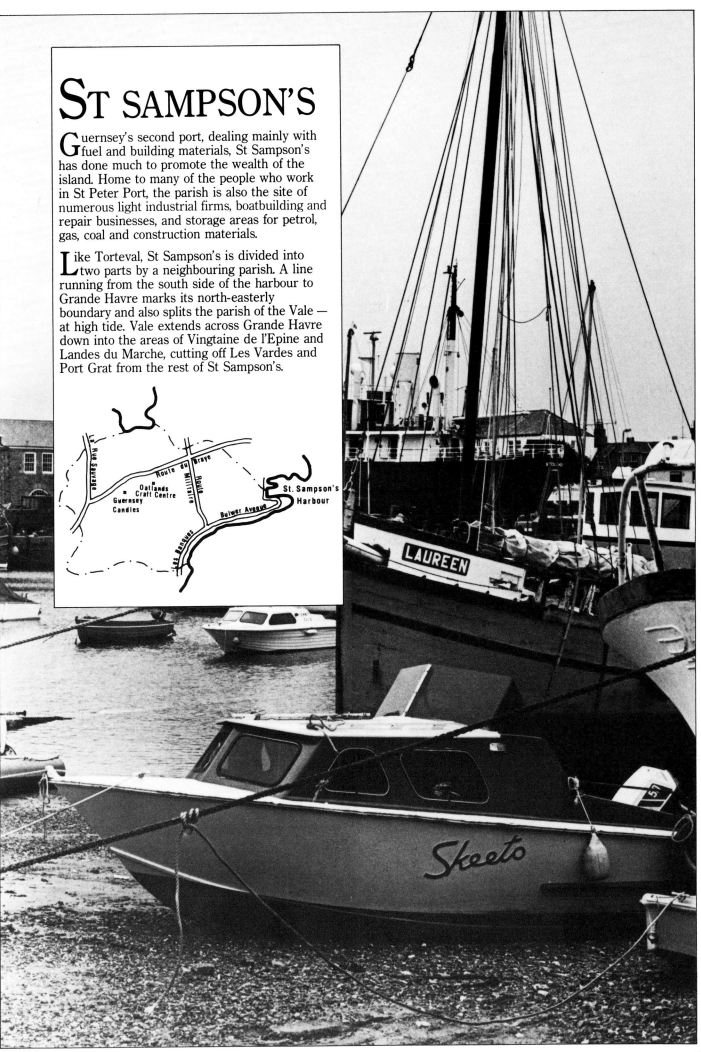

ST SAMPSON'S

Guernsey's second port, dealing mainly with fuel and building materials, St Sampson's has done much to promote the wealth of the island. Home to many of the people who work in St Peter Port, the parish is also the site of numerous light industrial firms, boatbuilding and repair businesses, and storage areas for petrol, gas, coal and construction materials.

Like Torteval, St Sampson's is divided into two parts by a neighbouring parish. A line running from the south side of the harbour to Grande Havre marks its north-easterly boundary and also splits the parish of the Vale — at high tide. Vale extends across Grande Havre down into the areas of Vingtaine de l'Epine and Landes du Marche, cutting off Les Vardes and Port Grat from the rest of St Sampson's.

OATLANDS CRAFT CENTRE

Perry's map ref: p.10 B2
Open: 10.00 - 5.30
Price guide: free; but small charge for bee section.
Bus route N

Now converted into workshops for glass blowers, potters, jewellery craftsmen and patchwork makers, the buildings of the Oatlands Craft Centre were originally part of a brickworks. Two of the original bottle-shaped kilns have been renovated, and inside one is a display showing the history of island brickmaking, together with examples of bricks manufactured by various local firms. In Napoleonic times, when the manufacture of bricks for the defence programme was of importance, the brickyard backed on to an inlet from the flooded Braye du Valle, and the building in which clay pots are now cast was the boatshed for craft which used the creek. The main building is roofed with a beautiful thatch put on in April 1983.

All the several businesses housed in the craft centre have flourishing export sales. Glass bottles are sold to French perfumeries, and glass paper weights grace desks all over the world. Patchwork aprons made in the centre are sold in Harrods, while the pottery chickens may be found in ovens as far apart as Singapore and Reykjavic.

Painting pottery

The glassware is finished in an engraving shop where any knobs and bumps are ground off. Here glasses, tankards and goblets can be engraved to order, and many local firms and sports clubs use the shop for gifts or trophies.

Two glass-sided beehives are the main attraction of a separate section devoted to the art and craft of bee-keeping. A small charge is made to go into this section, but it takes more than half an hour to complete the visit as the centre has made a video film showing how the hives were set up and maintained. Equipment used in bee-keeping, protective clothing, uses of wax and honey are all demonstrated.

Beehives on display

The glass furnaces are kept going for 11 months a year — worked by a shift system to ensure that maximum use is made of the huge amount of gas required to keep them hot. Two or three glassblowers working closely together swing the glass at temperatures of between 1200 and 1370 degrees centigrade between the furnaces and work stations. These near-molten pieces are rolled in coloured glass powder which mixes with the base to give a striped or diffused effect to the finished vase or paperweight.

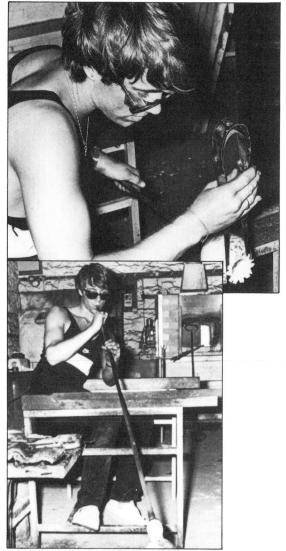

Blowing and shaping glass vases

The brick kilns

Next to the shop is the main pottery area where, each year, more than 20 tons of red earthenware clay from Stoke-on-Trent are made into 87,000 items. The potters can be watched from a viewing gallery as they make their salt-pigs, mugs, vases and plates, engrave names onto beakers and paint pottery before it is given the final glaze. In a separate section across the courtyard, other items are cast from liquid clay in moulds made of plaster of Paris. These dry the outside of each piece faster than the liquid centre which, after a time, is poured off leaving the object hollow.

After casting or turning on the potter's wheel, each piece is fired in a kiln to give a porous, matt, biscuit appearance. It is then sprayed with a 'tin glaze' which will later give the piece its base colour. This may be painted or etched — a technique known as sgraffito — before being sprayed with a glass-like glaze which gives the object a clear lustre when it is fired for a second time. A week's work, more than 1700 items, is put into the kiln for this final firing.

The highlight, however, is the hives in which the bees can be seen going about their daily business. The queen may be seen laying eggs, while worker bees fill empty cells with honey and seal them up. You can watch the scouting bees perform the dance which informs the hive where nectar and pollen producing flowers are to be found. The entrances to the hives are outside, but mirrors have been placed so that the bees can be seen coming in and out.

Beneath the bee room is a shop selling a range of natural goods, including local honey. Natural beauty preparations such as skin oil, herbal toner and wheatgerm night cream are on sale, all guaranteed free of artificial ingredients. Some are packed in pots made on the premises. Preserves and jams, 'like Gran used to make' are for sale along with mincemeat, pickles and marmalade from Clair's Kitchen. Guernsey-made perfume, local herbs and bees-wax candles are also for sale, and flowers and herbs can be posted to the UK for friends who warrant a little more than a postcard.

Two small converted stables in the thatched barn open off the main courtyard. The first houses a jewellery workshop where some of the items sold in some St Peter Port shops are made. The work is mostly chains, necklaces and earrings and each part of the finished product is made by hand. The workbench has a viewing gallery from where the two craftsmen can be seen and questioned. The jewellery can be bought from the craftsmen.

The second converted stable is full of patchwork made by seamstresses all over the island and on the premises. A 20th-century cottage industry has sprung up around the business, with many people working at home to supply the Oatlands centre. There is hardly room to move for pinafores, cushion covers, peg bags and little cloth mice. Many of the products are exported to outlets in London, New York and Paris, but they are also on sale in the shop at the centre.

Wandering around the centre may work up an appetite, which can be satisfied at the at the cafe on site, Clair's Guernsey Kitchen. The cafe has been mentioned in Egon Ronay's guide, and sells drinks, cakes, salads and hot snacks. There are also vegetarian and wholefood menus available. The cafe is decorated in country kitchen style with local prints on the walls, and during the summer meals and refreshments can be taken on to the front lawn to be eaten under shady umbrellas.

The Oatlands Craft Centre is primarily a workplace, and work does not stop to sell visitors the things being made. Many of the goods are for sale, however, in the Oatlands shop; there is also a section devoted to reject wares for those who like a bargain.

Guernsey Knitwear
M. W. Renouf Ltd.

The home of the Traditional guernsey

also   VALE PARISH GUERNSEY
ST. SAMPSON'S PARISH GUERNSEY
GUERNSEY CARDIGAN
and other HAND-MADE GARMENTS.

Send one home to your friends

6, The Bridge, St. Sampson's

Telephone: 0481 44487
(Mail orders)

Write or call in to see our superb PARISH design guernseys

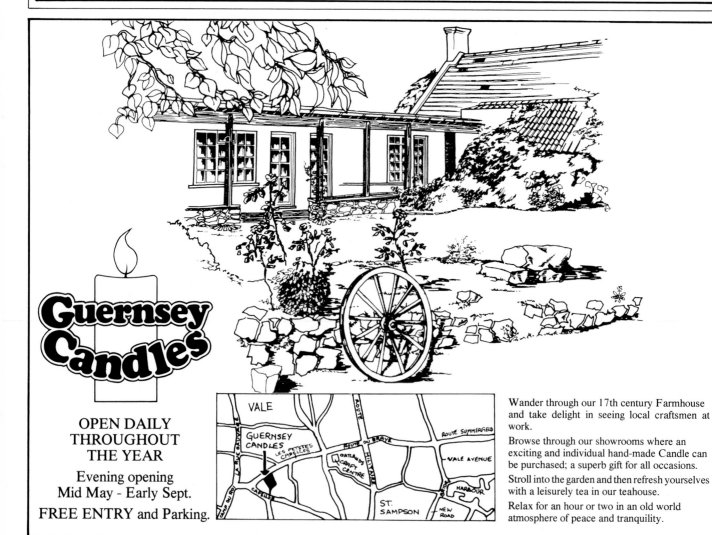

Guernsey Candles

OPEN DAILY THROUGHOUT THE YEAR

Evening opening
Mid May - Early Sept.

FREE ENTRY and Parking.

Wander through our 17th century Farmhouse and take delight in seeing local craftsmen at work.

Browse through our showrooms where an exciting and individual hand-made Candle can be purchased; a superb gift for all occasions.

Stroll into the garden and then refresh yourselves with a leisurely tea in our teahouse.

Relax for an hour or two in an old world atmosphere of peace and tranquility.

32

GUERNSEY CANDLES

Perry's map ref: p.9 G3
Open: summer
9.00 - 9.30 p.m.;
winter 9.00 - 5.30 daily
Price guide: free
Bus routes H1 and H2

Each year, more than 150,000 candles are produced by hand from 15 tons of paraffin wax in this cottage industry. The pure white wax is dyed and made into brilliantly-coloured candles which are then sold all over the world.

The business started 10 years ago in St Martin's, but it was too far from the beaten track moved to Les Petites Capelles in 1983. It began after founder Peter Martel returned to Guernsey with a £5 candle kit having seen a friend in the UK making them for charity. His first attempts were poor and he recycled the candles until he had made a few good ones. These were snapped up by visitors to his guest house, and he was encouraged to make more.

Pouring wax into a candle mould

The candles produced by carving can be 1ft high but most are between 6in and 9in. The wax in which they are dipped is kept at well below the boiling point of water, and although liquid it will not cause severe scalding if it drops on to the skin. It is also at this temperature when poured into moulds to make the cast candles. Spare wax is never wasted, as the off-cuts and drips are melted down to be used again.

The cafe behind the workshop

The business grew, and a few years later the guest house was sold. Guernsey Candles now employs five full-time staff and a few seasonal part-timers. In the first year fewer than 100 candles were made, but now nearly five times as many are made each day!

Visitors to the workshop can see two main techniques: the candles are either cast in moulds or dipped in hot wax and carved. This last method produces superb, unique candles. A basic core is dipped in different colours to give about 25 layers of soft warm wax. Before it cools the candle is sliced into with a sharp knife, producing slivers of different-coloured wax which are peeled back and woven into each other. Once they have cooled and set the candles are glazed. They are so beautiful that it is unlikely they are ever burnt!

The carving technique was started in the USA, but has been developed and refined in Guernsey to the extent that the candlemakers have become skilled artists in wax — training new recruits takes more than 18 months.

Moulds for the cast candles are made in the UK under licence to the Guernsey operation. They depict a wide range of subjects including dogs, eagles, clowns, and even a candle of the Last Supper! The biggest weighs over 14 lbs while the smallest is little more than a birthday cake candle.

The cast candles are literally hand painted. The artist dips her hands in the paint and rolls the candle like soap between them. This coats the upper surfaces but leaves the little wrinkles dark, giving the candle an appearance of depth.

Guernsey Candles has a licensed cafe on the site and snacks, salads and refreshments are available all day.

Peter Martel is justly proud of the business he has built up. He points out that while potteries are to be found in nearly every seaside town in Britain, the craft of candlemakers is unusual and intriguing. It combines art with function and produces unique items at a reasonable cost. His only problem is that the job has knocked some of the romance out of life — he hates candlelit dinners!

THE BRIDGE & ST SAMPSON'S HARBOUR

Guernsey was once in two parts. A shallow tidal channel, between 50 yards and half a mile wide, ran across the north splitting off the island of Clos du Valle. This channel is still known as the Braye du Valle and now houses hundreds of people as well as some highly productive farmland and vineries. The land was reclaimed by Sir John Doyle as part of a programme to upgrade the road system in 1806, paid for by the UK government. He was particularly worried that the French might land on the broad sands of L'Ancresse Bay at high tide, when the Militia would be unable to retaliate.

Before reclamation, much of the Braye du Valle was deep mud, and could not be crossed. The only place where access could be gained to the Clos du Valle at all stages of the tide was in St Sampson's where there was a bridge close to the parish church. A causeway ran from the Vale Church to L'Islet at the other end of the Braye but this could be used only at low tide. Doyle used both crossing places to dam the Braye thus reclaiming 300 acres of useful land. This was sold by the government for £5,000, and the money was given to the States of Guernsey to pay for new main roads from St Peter Port to Rocquaine and Vazon.

The Bridge retained its name but underwent a transformation, partly because of the effect the dam had on the creek which ran up to it. Boats had been moored at St Sampson's for centuries, sheltered by Mont Crevelt breakwater to the south-east and drying out on the muddy bottom at low tide before being loaded. Any mud scoured out of the creek by the tide was quickly replaced by more from the Braye, but once the Bridge was blocked this no longer happened and the mud quickly vanished — revealing sharp rocks which could easily pierce a ship's hull.

This was so dangerous that in 1820 a quay was built out from the north side of the creek to which the boats could tie up while being loaded. Used at first for the export of oysters, it became inadequate as the nearby granite quarrying industry grew up. A second quay was constructed parallel to the sandy south beach in front of the church. The area behind this quay was backfilled with ships' ballast and rubble, leaving the church 50 yards away from the sea. A jetty was pushed out northwards from the seaward end of the quay to protect ships from the beating they would otherwise receive when a heavy sea was running.

The Bridge was faced in stone to form a mooring. Granite work all round the harbour is of very high quality and is to be admired today. Besides the beautiful buildings, jetties and quays, even unlikely objects such as the bollards running around St Sampson's harbour are made from stone.

The North Quay was built along the remaining bay and backfilled with chalk, clay and stone ballast from the ships using the harbour. Disposal of ballast was a serious problem in the 19th century (modern ships pump water in and out of tanks) as it could soon choke the harbour, but this was solved in Guernsey by land reclamation projects below Vale Castle. The area between the two north piers is called Abraham's Bosom, a nautical name for the place where loaded ships could wait for favourable weather before sailing.

The yards grouped around the harbour, now converted to other uses, started as stone depots and crushing plants. The stone industry increased throughout the 19th century until in 1914 more than 400,000 tons were being exported annually. This needed a vast labour force, concentrated around the quarries which scarred the north of the island — thus starting the huge demand for housing in this area.

When the granite industry declined in the 1920s, due to the increasing use of modern materials for building and roadmaking, the fortunes of St Sampson's went down with it. The harbour started to be used mainly by fishing and pleasure boats, and the yards were converted to suit light industry, boatbuilding and engineering firms.

The area was important for shipbuilding during the 19th century, and many fine vessels were built between 1840 and 1897. One such was *Golden Spur* — at 656 tons, a full-rigged sailing ship, she was the largest to be built in Guernsey. Owned by a local firm, she was launched from Peter Ogier's yard in 1864 to ply between Britain and the Far East, only to be lost off Hong Kong in 1879.

After a period of some neglect following the building of the North Quay, the harbour became unable to cope with the demands of the stone trade. A railway to St Peter Port was considered, to enable easy export of granite from St Peter Port harbour. However, St Sampson's harbour was improved between 1860 and 1880 and the idea of a train was scrapped. Trams connected St Sampson's with 'the big city' instead.

In 1964, practically all the bulk cargoes were switched from St Peter Port, and the area south of St Sampson's harbour was developed as a storage site for oil, petrol, gas, building materials and fuel for the power station. This left St Peter Port free for passengers, container freight and the export of tomatoes.

During this century, the Bridge has remained one of the major routes to the northern parts of Guernsey. The attractive shops built on the land side of the road have living accommodation above them and the area has become a thriving shopping centre.

The shops were built by Mr Stonelake, who was a shipbuilder in the mid 1860s. His men worked on the houses when they had no other work — Stonelake referred to the Bridge as his 'hospital scheme', which could be returned to when necessary to avoid laying off workers. The floors of the houses were often made from old ships' timbers and although most have now been gutted and refloored, Tozer's the newsagent still has its original floorboards. Like the Mariners Arms pub, Tozer's has kept its original name.

At high tide the foundations of the shops are below sea level, while the houses behind would flood to their first floors without the protection of the road. This can be seen clearly by standing at the top of Commercial Road at high tide, and comparing the water level in the harbour with the houses at the bottom of the hill leading away from the Bridge.

The creek and harbour were originally protected by two forts. The Vale Castle dominates the view to the north, and to the south protection was offered by a smaller fortification at Mont Crevelt. It was one of 15 round towers, built in the 1780s for £100 each. It stands on a small hill surrounded by reclaimed land.

The Crocq, a jetty built out from the southern quay of the harbour, is always worth a closer look. It is used to beach boats for the winter or for repairs, so there is always something of interest to catch the eye. A clock tower stands close to the road, above the harbourmaster's office, while a 27ft-high obelisk, inscribed with the names of the 1872 States Labour Committee who were responsible for having the Crocq built, can be seen in the centre. A menhir, uprooted from elsewhere, stands close to the slip at the entrance to the Crocq and is inscribed as a monument to Daniel De Lisle Brock, Bailiff from 1821 to 1842.

The harbour with The Bridge in the background

ST SAMPSON'S CHURCH

Perry's map ref: P.11 F3

This is the oldest church in the Bailiwick and stands near the spot where St Sampson — the first Christian to preach on the island — landed on Guernsey in the sixth century. Born in Llantwit Major, South Wales, St Sampson founded the abbey of Dol in Brittany in AD 550, and was given the oversight of the Channel Islands. When he visited Guernsey he landed on the shore of the natural harbour which bears his name, and is said to have built a little chapel or oratory on the site of the present church. Nothing remains of the original building, although it is mentioned in a document of 1054.

inscribed in French, which tells how Thomas Falla, aged 18, died at the seige of Seringapatam in southern India on 6 April 1799. He was hit in the thigh by a solid cannon ball weighing 26 pounds. It seems that as he was carried off the battlefield alive, his leg was terribly swollen and he appeared to weigh more on one side than the other. The explanation only came after his death six hours later, when the cannon ball was discovered in the wound which had closed up around it!

On either side of the altar hang the old colours of the Guernsey Militia's North Regiment, placed there after new colours were presented to the regiment during Queen Victoria's jubilee in 1887. The two flags on either side of the chancel are from the Royal Guernsey Militia and have recently been restored and rehung. In the south chapel above the entrance to the vestry, is the church organ. This was moved from the north chapel, which was opened

The earliest reference to the present Church of St Sampson appears in the records of Coutances Bishopric in Normandy, dated 23 March 1510. Before the quays of St Sampson's harbour were built the church stood almost on the seashore at the foot of a small hill. At high water the sea would come up to the churchyard wall, and during spring tides the water flowed along the road (then much lower than it is today) at the side of the church. Today it is hidden behind warehouses built on the south side of the harbour.

The church consists of a nave with two chapels on either side of the chancel. A pyramidal saddle-back tower stands mid-way down the church at the end of the nave; dating from the early Norman period, it is one of the oldest parts of the building. The gable above the main entrance has two nice features. Corbie (crow or raven) steps run down the gable and the bottom greyish stone is a sundial — the scoring can be seen when viewed from the south. Older people of St Sampson's are said to have learned to tell the time from the sundial.

Six steps lead down into the nave from the main entrance, a traditional feature of Guernsey churches, and a flight of stairs runs up to a gallery overlooking the nave and chancel. Over the priest's stall is a marble tablet,

up in the process, allowing the true proportions of the building's architecture to be appreciated.

There are several stained glass windows in the church, including a coloured light over the gallery in memory of Reverend Robert Jones, rector from 1892 to 1909. Others show the Resurrection, St Peter's attempt to walk on water, the Virgin Mary and St John, the Good Shepherd and Good Samaritan, a Madonna and child, and Christ teaching a child. The most recent window depicts St Sampson of Dol and is in memory of Canon E.L. Frossard who was rector and dean for 50 years from 1918 to 1958. He was the father of Guernsey's current Bailiff, Sir Charles Frossard.

The churchyard is one of the best kept in the islands, and is planted with a variety of lovely shrubs. Part of the churchyard tragically fell into the Longue Hougue Quarry in 1969, and the area has needed extensive work, complicated by the laws relating to graves, to restore it to its present condition. Benches have been placed in a position overlooking the quarry, and it is a quiet and pleasant place to sit, well away from the rush and bustle of St Sampson's town.

Vale

This is one of the largest parishes both in area and population. At one time it included the whole of the Clos du Valle, then a separate island, and part of mainland Guernsey. Reclamation of the Braye du Valle, the narrow channel which separated the two parts of the parish, might have joined them but the land was deemed part of St Sampson's parish which now splits the Vale in two.

Many industries are based in the parish. These range from boatbuilding and engineering firms around the harbour to the island's power station. Many specialised companies are based on industrial estates in the area.

These use a workforce which first moved into the parish for the granite industry, which has left the Vale pock-marked with quarries. The stone was exported and used extensively in the road-building schemes of the 19th century. The better-quality granite was used for parts of public buildings which suffer hard wear, such as the steps of St Paul's Cathedral in London.

Vale residents enjoy the best weather on the island, as much of the parish is flat and close to sea level. It does not attract the cloud and mist that the higher parishes occasionally experience. The States Tourist Board collect their official weather figures from a private station on L'Ancresse!

BORDEAUX HARBOUR

There can be no nicer natural harbour in the Channel Islands than Bordeaux, especially at high tide. So inspiring is it that Victor Hugo set much of his book *Les Travailleurs de la Mer (The Toilers of the Sea)* at the spot.

The haven is used by fishermen as a mooring and by divers interested in the abundant marine life in the area. Many islanders learn to swim there. At high tide two jetties on the south side of the harbour are just covered by the water and make excellent stages for diving. Between the jetties and a rock 25 yards north, the bathing is safe, but wicked currents run around the northern part of Guernsey and elsewhere in the area swimming is very dangerous.

These islands, or at least the waters off them, are often the destination of the many private fishermen whose boats are moored in Bordeaux. There they fish with pots for crabs and lobsters, rod and line for bream, bass, whiting and flatfish, or feather for mackerel. Bargain hunters can often buy fish cheaply by approaching the fishermen as they step ashore.

To the south of the harbour a pleasant beach stretches to the base of Vale Castle. At the southern end of the beach is a kiosk with conveniences, for the area is very popular during the summer months.

Two small islands are accessible from the north of Bordeaux at low tide. Houmet Benest, which forms part of the northern arm of the natural harbour, is closest to the top of the beach and can be walked to most of the time. Paradis, a little further north, is at the bottom of the beach and can only be reached at low tide. It is looked after by the National Trust of Guernsey and is used by fishermen who allow themselves to be cut off by the tide.

Birdwatchers too find the area of interest. The beaches and the muddy harbour bottom attract many waders, while the bottleneck between Bordeaux and Herm causes oceanic species to approach the island more closely. Sea pies or oystercatchers nest on both the islets and visitors are asked not to stay too long in the spring and early summer.

BEAUCETTE MARINA

It comes as no surprise that one of Guernsey's major leisure occupations is boating. Locally-born islanders are said to have salt in their veins, while those who adopt the island often do so to get access to the excellent sailing and boating. There are more than 2500 registered small boats in Guernsey and mooring them has become a great problem. St Peter Port has two marinas and as this book is written £13 million is being spent building a third.

Perhaps the most interesting marina, however, is found half a mile north of Bordeaux Harbour, close to Fort Doyle. The site was created during the quarrying industry boom when the extraction of diorite, a greenish granite, created a large hole. When the quarry was abandoned the hole was very deep, and separated from the sea by a wall and narrow strip of land.

In private ownership, the quarry was made into a marina, with access at half tide upwards, by the Royal Engineers who came to a neat arrangement with the proprietor. In exchange for food and accommodation they would blast an entrance through to the sea as a training exercise. It was expected to take a few days but the plan went badly wrong and the men were in Guernsey for more than nine months!

Because the marina is almost completely surrounded by the old quarry walls it is always sheltered, and provides one of the best moorings in Guernsey. The land around is about 30ft above sea level and only the tips of the tallest masts are visible, even at high tide.

The Channel Islands Yacht Marina has an office at the top of a white building which stands on the edge of the quarry. There is an excellent and very popular restaurant beneath it.

Vale Castle

Perry's map ref: p.11 G2

At one time the hill on which this castle stands was the only place of refuge available to the inhabitants of the Clos du Valle at all stages of the tide. These islanders, separated from the rest of Guernsey by the Braye du Valle, needed somewhere to fortify against attack, and by 600 B.C., during the early Iron Age, the site had been developed into a hillfort.

The fort was added to later, but the only medieval remains are close to the west wall, discovered during excavations in 1980. According to the Ancient Monuments Committee, who have referred to documents of the time, the fort was extended during the 16th and 17th centuries.

A path leads up opposite a car park on the coast road north of St Sampson's harbour. The road continues in a long left bend which sweeps around the castle to Bordeaux Harbour.

The path up to the castle takes you under a gateway with a portcullis, leading into the fort. To the left of the path, on the slope leading to the main entrance, is a tiny cemetery which contains the graves of Russian troopers. Some 6,000 soldiers were quartered in the barracks at Vale in 1799, following a battle in Holland during the Napoleonic Wars. The Russians were not allowed into England because of clauses in the Bill of Rights which prohibited foreign troops. A disease contracted in the Dutch marches carried off several hundred who were buried in a field close by. Their remains were finally laid to rest under the battlements some time later.

Barracks built inside the castle walls in the late eighteenth century were used for local housing between the two world wars, but they were pulled down in 1945 leaving a magazine as the only building in the fort. In front of it is an old, sealed well.

Other signs of occupation inside the fort are several cobbled barrack roads, the uneven surfaces of which require great care when walking over them, and concrete from the German presence in the war. These last invaders fortified the castle, putting in a large gun emplacement and several machine-gun nests, the sites of which can be visited and explored.

The view from the battlements is one of the most interesting in the island. Due to Guernsey's hill structure, churches as far apart as St Martin's, Castel, Cobo and the Vale can be seen. Panoramic sea views take the eye from Les Casquets Reef in the north, past Ortac and Burhou, to Alderney. The view then takes in France, the Humps, a line of rocky islets north of Herm, and Jethou. Behind these islands are Sark and Jersey.

The battlements also look down on some of the light industry of the Vale, situated in La Hure Mare Industrial Estate. The power station chimneys dominate the area and while everyone criticises their appearance, not a single light switch has been turned off in protest. A crenellated tower and chimney to the south mark the entrance to what was a stone works; today the yard is used for the warehousing of building materials and boat manufacture.

The long approach path, like the rest of the site, was repaired and renovated in 1983 as a relief work scheme for unemployed youngsters. Other parts, renovated in the project, run around the outside of the battlements linking several picnic sites.

L'ANCRESSE COMMON WALK

Over the sticks at L'Ancresse

Perry's map ref: p.6 B4

This walk is about two and a half miles long, mostly on the flat, and will take about an hour. It starts at the children's playground car park at Les Amarreurs, goes around Chouet Headland to Pembroke and on past L'Ancresse Bay to Bunker Hill. Doubling back you will pass Rocque Balan hill before joining the racecourse track which leads back to the start, via Les Fouaillages archaeological site.

Your arrival at the car park is best timed to coincide with high tide, as the little harbour at Les Amarreurs, with its breakwater which juts out into Grande Havre Bay, looks its best at this time.

Set off northwards along the top of a 20ft cliff which forms the junction between the windblown dunes of the common and the white sand of Ladies Bay and Chouet Beach. The beach is the site of autocross meetings during the summer.

Aiming for the big German pillbox on the hill, continue north past the Chouet car park where there are toilets, including facilities for the disabled, and a cafe. A path leading off to the left can be taken if you want to extend the walk. It leads around the headland passing several old quarries, one of which is full of black oil washed ashore after the wreck of the *Torrey Canyon* near the Scilly Isles in 1967. Follow the path until the German bunker is sighted once more.

The golf course

If you have not made a detour, follow the main road by the Chouet car park, up over a slight rise. Turn right towards the German pillbox at the entrance to Mont Cuet quarry which was the main source of granite for the North Beach marina in St Peter Port.

As you go over the top of the hill past the pillbox you get a magnificent view of the common, golf course and northern part of Guernsey. The Vale Church can be seen behind the start of your walk while in front of you is a 40ft drop into La Hougue Biart quarry, now flooded. Follow the lane (Les Hures) down the other side of the hill, past the golf practice course. The lane wanders on past a slipway down to Baie de la Jaonneuse to reach a little complex of buildings at Pembroke Bay.

The main buildings are The Pembroke Bay Hotel and the two golf clubs which use the course — the Royal Guernsey and L'Ancresse Golf Clubs. The hotel is also a centre for wind-surfing, which can be watched from the huge concrete wall built by the Germans during the Occupation. It is easy to see why they and military men at the turn of the eighteenth century were worried about seaborne attack across this beach.

Follow the coast wall along a path which runs parallel to the beach. As it reaches the far end, head inland along a narrow lane which skirts the bottom of Bunker Hill. When this lane reaches the main road, turn right towards a gorse-covered hillock. This is Rocque Balan, which has two ancient cup-markings on its flat top. There are usually a few tame goats tethered here, and they love a bit of fuss. L'Ancresse common is used by residents of the Clos du Valle for grazing their animals, and the golf course must be one of the few to have cattle tethered on the rough between the fairways.

The main road leads down to the L'Ancresse crossroads. The Pembroke complex can be seen to your right while the Vale Church is again in sight on the left. Cross the road and turn on to a wide path which runs parallel to the main road, separated from the golf course by gorse banks. The path doubles as a racecourse for horses two or three times a year. Follow the path, which turns right after some 300 yards, until you reach the children's playground once more. Just before you reach the end of your walk, the path passes a sign for Les Fouaillages, one of the archaeological sites described on page

ARCHAEOLOGICAL SITES

Le Dehus

Recent excavations indicate that man has been exploring Guernsey for at least 7,000 years, possibly longer, without a guide book such as this! The evidence for this came to light one day in the hot, dry summer of 1976 when John Lihou, a member of La Societe Guernesiaise archaeological section, found a granite slab sticking up from an interesting mound on L'Ancresse, uncovered by an accidental gorse fire. He had been aware of the site for some years, but an opportunity to investigate it closely did not occur until after the fire.

The site, now known as Les Fouaillages, was excavated by Dr Ian Kinnes, for the States Ancient Monuments Committee, with the voluntary help of La Societe Guernesiaise. He found that it had a complicated history. Middle Stone Age flint tools showed that the site was first used between 6,000 and 5,000 BC. A triangular burial mound measuring 66 by 33ft was built later; dated to about 4,500 BC, it is the oldest-known stone structure in Europe. 1,500 years later, during the late Stone Age, the mound was carefully covered with earth and stones, and around 2,500 BC a further monument was erected on top of this enlarged mound. In the early Bronze Age, during which time there was a settlement next to the site, the mound was again carefully covered,

to remain largely undisturbed until its excavation. Les Fouaillages is now preserved and well signposted from Les Amarreurs Road, L'Ancresse.

This is not the only Stone Age burial site on the islands. Guernsey and Herm abound with cists and chambered tombs of varying types, all of which are worth a visit. Many were excavated in the early and mid 19th century by Frederick Lukis. He rescued much of the material from the attentions of local quarrymen who saw easy pickings to be had from the huge pieces of granite which were used for many of the tombs. His large collection of local archaeological material is now held by Guernsey Museum.

La Varde passage grave on the high hill between Pembroke bus terminus and Chouet car park is the most impressive of these Stone Age monuments, being more than 40ft long and 12ft wide. In it were found burials from two periods, separated by piles of limpets. There were more than 30 heaps of bones, including the remains of several individuals and bones of at least one child.

A small group of cist-in-circles can be found a few yards inland from L'Ancresse Bay, close to a pool called La Mare es Mauves. A stone found lying close by has a small cross carved on it and may be a Christianised menhir.

Les Fouaillages

Another northern tomb is to be found at Le Dehus, off La Rochelle Road, Vale. You can get inside the grave, which is lit by electric lights, and see the chambers which branch off the main tunnel. It is the most spectacular tomb in the island with a unique carved figure and carvings on one of the capstones.

Le Creux es Faies, off La Rue du Braye, St Peter's, is another tomb which can be entered. This is said locally to be the door to fairyland and there are many superstitious people who will not go near the place, especially after dark. There were few finds when the tomb was excavated, possibly because it had been used as a place where soldiers would hide to avoid work parties. It was later sealed by one of their officers. The main finds were dated 2000 - 1800 BC, and included a Samian sherd, now on display in the Guernsey Museum, beaker pottery and two barbed and tanged arrowheads.

Evidence of Bronze Age occupation of Guernsey is scarce as most of the tumuli mounds were destroyed in the 19th century, but the huge defensive structures at Jerbourg Point include earthworks dating to the earliest part of this era. Excavations have revealed a small, stone-faced rampart, barbed and tanged arrowheads and pottery typical of the period.

This fort is part of extensive earthworks which make up the largest archaeological site in the Channel Islands. Three Iron Age phases are represented, together with medieval remains and a World War Two fortification. The site stretches across the headland for more than 850 yards but the centre portion has been destroyed by modern development. At the eastern end, above Divette, the fort's ramparts are well preserved, and tower over the head of anyone standing in one of the ditches.

Aerial photography during the drought of 1976 revealed strange shapes in a field at Les Tranquesous, St Saviour's, which turned out to be the remains of a late Iron Age settlement. This had an enclosure, huts and what appear to have been three tiny fields. Another Iron Age site on the outskirts of St Peter Port, at King's Road, produced pottery of the French La Tene style similar to that found at Hengistbury Head in southern England.

Until recently there was little evidence of Roman settlement in Guernsey — a few coins had been picked up, but little else. However, a Roman building has recently been discovered in La Plaiderie, St Peter Port, and two wrecks have been found on the seabed just outside the entrance to the harbour. Both are thought to be Roman galleys, and one is complete, though buried. Marine archaeologist Margaret Rule, who raised the Tudor galleon *Mary Rose,* is looking at ways of raising one of the wrecks as this book goes to print.

Le Dehus

VALE POND

Perry's map ref: P.6 B5

Parking: over the road at the northern end of L'Islet

Bus routes: L1 and L2

Owned by St Peter Port wine and spirit merchants Bucktrouts, this pond, with its saltmarsh habitat — unique in Guernsey — has been set up as a nature reserve named after one of Bucktrouts' former directors, the late Colin McCathie. It is managed by La Societe Guernesiaise whose members keep the area clean, look after a birdwatching hide and monitor the plants, animals, birds and insects which are found there. Mr McCathie was a past president of the society, and an expert on the area, its drainage and general history.

Vale Pond is all that remains of the Braye du Valle, a narrow channel which ran from Grande Havre to St Sampson's harbour, which was reclaimed under the orders of General Doyle in 1806. A barrier was build across Le Pont St Michel, a set of stepping stones, connecting the pond to the other side of the channel, creating the sandy and popular beach at L'Islet.

A road was built across the dyke which is high enough to afford views down the Braye to St Sampson's harbour. Strangely for Guernsey, the view ends at distant wooded hills. These are the tops of the neighbouring islands, Herm and Jethou; the four miles of sea between them and Guernsey cannot be seen.

'Even if you pass the Vale Pond every half hour . . . always check it' is the advice in a local guide book given to bird watchers visiting the island. It may well be followed by everyone, for there is always something going on there.

On the left-hand side of the pond is an extensive area of *Phragmites* reed which is home to one of the largest colonies of reed warblers in Guernsey. These tiny birds winter south of the Sahara in Africa, but come to Guernsey to breed. One pair has been recorded nesting within inches of the same site for 12 years! During the spring and summer they can be heard singing a scratchy song from the tops of the reed stems.

They are not the only birds from distant parts to visit the Vale Pond. It acts as a huge transport cafe for migrants which stop to feed and rest on their long journeys north or south. To the right of the reed bed is a big expanse of mud and low sedge which attracts wading birds of all sorts. A few resident moorhens and coots breed on the pond but their numbers are swollen greatly during the winter by birds which come in from Holland — the snipe, greenshank, common sandpiper and redshank are all common. In the autumn, birds such as buff-breasted and pectoral sandpipers arrive at the site, having been blown over the Atlantic by gales from the Caribbean. Grey herons and kingfishers can also be seen on occasion.

Birdwatchers have two places to watch from. They either use a hide provided by a local charitable trust, or look over the 6ft high wall between the road and the pond. Designed to provide access for wheelchairs, the hide has an entrance through a gap in the wall, but a few yards up the road, towards the church, a low stone conveniently placed to stand on allows good views from the wall itself over the whole area.

The pond is connected by an underground pipe to Grande Havre on the other side of the road. A pumping station in the granite building opposite the entrance to the hide removes excess water in times of flood, but most of the time the water is free to go up or down the pipe depending on the relative levels. So, on high tides sea water floods into the pond bringing with it some quite large fish such as grey mullet, flounders and bass. These can often be seen dappling the surface.

The muddy areas beside the pond are reached by going through a gate at the west end of the wall. You should do this only if you are a keen botanist, as the going is very soft and disturbance should be kept to a minimum. Sea aster, halberd-leafed orache, sea hard grass and sea club-rush can be found. Take care not to fall into any of the deep ditches that criss-cross the area.

Salt water also seeps into the pond through the bank on which the road is built. Between the base of the wall and the pond there is a white deposit of salt where the sea water has evaporated. The bank is home to woody tree lupins, from which the domestic varieties of the flower were developed. Yarrow, wall rocket, sea radish and bittersweet can also be found growing here. Other plants include sea beet, rock samphire, tree mallow and pink oxalis.

L'ANCRESSE BAY

Perry's map refs: p.6 C1, C2, D2, E2.
Bus routes L1 or L2 to Pembroke terminus.

Much of the island's northern road system was created or improved because of the vulnerability of this flat sandy beach to invasion. The threat seemed so great in 1800 that the Lieutenant-Governor Sir John Doyle decided something had to be done. His big fear was that an invading army could attack at high tide, and the defending militia would be unable to retaliate across the then tidal Braye du Valle for some hours. This would give the attackers time to dig in. During a debate at the time Doyle could not say whether he was a general or an admiral, for the state of the tide would determine if the ensuing battle would be military or naval!

L'Ancresse is said to have been named because Robert, Duke of Normandy, anchored there after a fruitless attempt to invade England in 1031. The bay is an easy landing place, which is why it is surrounded with forts and Napoleonic towers. It is a strange thought that although the weapons of war alter very rapidly, strategies do not. The Germans felt the need to fortify the beach-head against tanks during their occupation of Guernsey.

The north-west corner of L'Ancresse Bay is called Pembroke, and it is here that both the sand and easy landing for boats combine to attract vast numbers of holiday makers each year. It is one of the most popular sandy bays for families, and the sheltered waters attract the attention of modern invaders — windsurfers. A windsurfing school and centre is based at the Pembroke Hotel.

Accordingly he ordered the Braye to be reclaimed, and immediately built the long straight road to the Vale Church and onwards to L'Ancresse Bay. His 14ft-wide roads can be easily recognised today. Not only were they relatively straight when compared with the medieval lanes connecting the villages, parishes and tiny fields, but they also had footpaths, many of which survive.

The military roads built by Doyle ran through nearly every parish on the island and connected St Peter Port with outlying places such as Rocquaine, Cobo and the Vale. They were marked by granite milestones which gave the distance from the Town Church. 26 remain on seven of the routes, built into walls or free-standing. The miles are marked in Roman numerals. The roads opened up trade, and although initially resisted by local people they were finally welcomed by the various parochial authorities.

Sea anglers enjoy good sport with mackerel, bass, pollack and flatfish from the headlands on either side of the bay. Bait is usually ragworm or lugworm dug from the beaches, or sandeels bought fresh or frozen from the fish market. Various competitions are run throughout the year for specimen fish caught by both local and visiting anglers.

L'Ancresse Bay has kiosks which sell refreshments and beach goods at both ends of the beach. There is a public telephone and bus terminus at Pembroke.

FORT LE MARCHANT

Victorian gun-track, Fort Le Marchant

Fort Le Marchant:
Perry's map ref: p.7 F1

Fort Doyle:
Perry's map ref: p.7 H1

If Pleinmont is known in Guernsey as Land's End, then Fort Le Marchant must surely be the island's John O'Groats. It is the most northerly point and forms the apex of Guernsey's roughly triangular shape. A rifle range on the headland tends to keep people away, but unless the warning flags are up the area is well worth a visit.

If you are going by car, drive down Rue de la Fontenelle between the gorse-covered slopes of Grande Hougue on your left and Hougue Patris to the right. Park at the end of the lane which runs past the fourth of the towers built in the 1780s, at Le Catelain. The tower has a flagpole which is used to show when the rifle range is in use.

A path runs from the car park out to Fort Le Marchant which was named after Major-General John Le Marchant. He was described by his headmaster at boarding school in Bath as the greatest dunce he had ever met, but Le Marchant went on to found the Royal Military College, at Sandhurst, and had a sparkling army career.

The Victorian facade of the fort was pulled down in recent years, revealing the Napoleonic defences at its core. It has been reinforced twice in recent times, once by the Germans, who mounted six guns on the old ramparts. The mountings for these can still be seen, togther with tracks for the Victorian guns made from carved blue granite. The most recent reinforcements are two huge earth banks which house and act as backdrops for the rifle range targets. The mechanisms by which the targets are raised and lowered can be inspected.

At the end of the headland, in the fort, you are almost completely surrounded by water and have a view which takes in six of the 18th century towers built in the area. Fort Doyle is to the east with Alderney on the horizon north of it. To the west, the whole of L'Ancresse Bay can be seen with a view across part of the common to Grande Havre and Rousse.

FORT DOYLE

Part of the track leading from Fort Le Marchant to this headland was made by German troops during the Occupation for their light railway, which ran around much of the coast of Guernsey. Fort Doyle was built to guard the entrance to the Little Russel, the stretch of water between Guernsey and Herm. Like the defensive towers, this mid 19th century fort could not have withstood the gun power of the era in which it was built. Designed to look something like a child's model fort, the defences were of little use until the Germans reinforced the place with their characteristic concrete.

Fort Doyle is the site at which the undersea telephone cable comes ashore. It runs between the island and Bournemouth, part of the complex communications system on which the island, and in particular the finance industry, relies. Occasionally cut by trawlers' netting equipment, it is backed up by microwave links via Jersey.

Fort Doyle

Some of the best angling in Guernsey is to be enjoyed from the rocks on the headland. The water inshore is very deep and anglers can cast on to sand from some of the rocks. This gives them a range of quarry from flatfish such as plaice and sole, through conger, bass, pollack and wrasse to mid-water feeders such as mackerel and garfish.

From the headland on a clear day there is a fine view of Les Casquets Reef to the north, round past Alderney, the French coast, Herm and Sark, to Jersey. Closer to shore, east of the headland, is the lighthouse on Platte Fougere.

Shingle bank, Fort Doyle

CASTEL

Castel is the largest parish in Guernsey. It is dominated by the remains of a huge marsh called La Grande Mare, formed by water trapped between the bottom of an escarpment which runs from Castel to the south-west corner of Guernsey, and sand dunes thrown up by the prevailing winds across Vazon Bay. La Grande Mare has largely been drained now, and many of the rare plants, insects and birds which were once found there have disappeared.

Vazon is one of the most popular beaches on the island, not only for swimmers and sunbathers, but also because it has a stretch allocated to surfers and is a place where horse riders can gallop their mounts hard for some distance.

The Castel parish church is the site of a statue-menhir which stands to the left of the west porch. Found inside the church in the late 19th century, it is a strangely compelling example of prehistoric human representation. Marks around the top are thought to represent a head-band, the front is graced by a U-shaped necklace and a girdle has been carved half way up the back. The figure represented is female and the right breast has been deliberately damaged.

LE FRIQUET BUTTERFLY CENTRE

Perry's map ref: p.16 A3
Open: summer only,
9.00 - 6.00
Price guide C
Bus routes F and G

A visit to one of the greenhouses at Le Friquet will provide you with a unique sight. It is the only such place in Guernsey where the grower encourages weeds, and takes pride in the fact that his plants are decimated by insects. In fact, the weeds are necessary to produce the insects — the crop of caterpillars which eventually hatch into butterflies that are famous throughout the world.

Most of the butterfly centres which have sprung up all over the UK, and perhaps even the practice of releasing insects bred in captivity, have been inspired by Le Friquet. Guernsey's Butterfly Centre was the first place where the public could walk among free-flying tropical and British species, learning about their life-cycles, host plants and caterpillars.

The idea was the brainchild of David Lowe who, when the tomato industry went into decline, looked for alternative uses for green-houses. At the time Le Friquet was one of the island's major flower producers and had been opened to the public to show the commercial methods of growing garden favourites such as chrysanthemums and freesias.

The butterflies were a later innovation. They are kept in one of the greenhouses which has fine netting pinned under the glass, allowing air and light through while keeping the insects secure. A double door allows access, and once inside the visitor is free to wander while hundreds of beautiful butterflies flutter by.

Some species are bred at Le Friquet, but the majority are brought in from tropical countries as chrysalids which are cooled for the journey. The warmth of the greenhouse is sufficient to make them hatch, and soon the spectacular creatures are flying freely among the visitors and plants. The latter include many species which are chosen because the butterflies will lay their eggs on them or feed from the nectar in their flowers. Thus you will see willow bushes which have been ravaged by Camberwell beauty caterpillars, banks of nettles for painted ladies to lay their eggs on and milkweed for the monarch butterfly. Once they hatch, the buddleia and Michaelmas daisy flowers attract and help to feed them.

Sugar solution is fed to the butterflies from glass reservoirs on which brightly coloured, artificial flowers are attached, attracting the butterflies. The solution dribbles slowly to the centre of these plastic blooms where the insects sip it from cotton wool. The butterflies are attracted to all bright colours, and many women in floral dresses have found that the butterflies settle on them in the hope of finding nectar!

In other parts of the greenhouse, chrysalids are stored in rows while they hatch. The butterflies can be seen emerging, their wings spreading out into fantastic shapes and colours,

Comma and common blue

as blood is pumped into them. The blood vessels dry up once the wings are formed.

As you walk along the paths inside the green-house, some dead butterflies will be noticed on the ground. The insects are short-lived, dying soon after they breed. None of the butterflies bred at Le Friquet are killed and mounted — they all live out their alloted span as the objects of admiration and wonder.

Heliconius melpomone

In another greenhouse you can inspect a collection of insects and similar creatures which is not for the squeamish. Seven-inch tarantulas and bird-eating spiders — some alive in special cages and others mounted on display — are among the captives. They are, of course, quite safe, and the little collection is fascinating. It includes leaf insects, which many children have kept as pets, and a colony of leaf-cutting ants. These huge insects can be seen carrying large pieces of leaf over their heads as they cross a tree trunk bridge which connects their nest to the artificial feeding site.

Le Friquet has an excellent shop for locally-made goods and souvenirs, as well as a cafe and a gravel-floored restaurant. This is the venue for the increasingly popular sport of boule, the French form of bowls. Games are held in the evening and there are hopes of starting a local boule league.

MARTELLO TOWERS

Fort Saumarez: a true Martello tower capped by a German battery

True Martello towers were built on top of much older forts at the Cup and Saucer, Rocquaine, and at Fort Saumarez, L'Eree. This tower is now capped by a German battery. At Fort Hommet, on the headland between Vazon and Albecq, a later fort was demolished after the Occupation to reveal the red granite Martello tower behind it.

A pleasant afternoon can be spent hunting for the 15 towers. In doing so you will enjoy a good drive and see much of the island. Head north along the coast road from St Peter Port. Towers one and two have unfortunately been demolished — the site of tower one is opposite the tramsheds at the Red Lion road filter, while tower two was opposite Belgrave Flats at the Halfway. Tower three is still standing at Mont Crevelt, St Sampson's.

Tower four is at Fort Le Marchant on one of the most northern points of the island, while L'Ancresse Common is the site of the next batch. Number five is just to the north of a car park at the west end of L'Ancresse Bay, while towers six and seven are behind the bay along the sixteenth fairway of the golf course.

Number eight has been demolished, but stood on La Varde Hill overlooking Pembroke Bay. Tower nine is on a sharp left-hand bend a few yards north of Pembroke Hotel. The tenth tower is on the south side of Chouet headland between two old granite quarries, while number eleven is on Rousse Point at Les Dicqs headland.

Vazon Bay was protected by tower twelve, a well-known landmark which is the starting point for car and motorcycle sprints during the summer. Tower thirteen is also a local landmark standing above Petit Bot Bay. It can be looked at from above, giving a clear view of the well in the roof, from the cliff path which rises up the hill towards Le Gouffre.

Tower fourteen is quite hard to find, as you have to walk down to Saints Bay where it guards the beachhead. Number fifteen is best reached by boat as it too guards a beach, at Fermain Bay. The boat ride from St Peter Port drops you at the base of the tower which stands at the top of an impressive sea wall.

Commonly called Martello towers after the similar forts on the Kent and Sussex coasts, the 15 circular towers built in Guernsey during the 1780s are in fact of a different and earlier design from the English structures, which were designed after a fight between two British warships and a gun tower on Mortella Point, Corsica, in 1794.

It is fortunate that Guernsey's towers were never tested in battle, for they would not have been strong enough to cope with attack by the cannon of the era. True Martello towers are broader in relation to their height, with sloping reinforced sides and a much stronger construction. Most of the Guernsey towers have two storeys, vertical sides and a diameter of little more than 20ft. There is no doubt that very little force would be needed to knock them down. Each cost between £100 and £156 to build and builders' invoices for some of them are held by Guernsey Museum.

A locally-designed tower with magazine

FOLK MUSEUM AND SAUMAREZ PARK

Perry's map ref: p.15 G1
Open: April to October,
9.00 - 5.00
Price guide B
Bus routes F and N

In a corner, between the hearth and kitchen window, stands the green bed, a rectangular, wooden-framed couch on which a green baize cushion, stuffed with bracken, dried rushes and chaff is placed. This was used for extra seating during family get-togethers or special occasions. A large table takes up much of the space on one side of the room, while in some kitchens, a pump and granite trough occupied the other. Hanging from the ceiling is a rack for bacon or bread, baskets and other utensils which would otherwise get in the way.

Similar scenes of Guernsey life are to be seen in the other areas of the museum. You will wonder how the old bedroom compares with today's for comfort, or at the exertions which went into ploughing, seaweed gathering and making cider, which was the usual refreshment. The tools used for many country crafts are on display, including a cider apple crusher and press, and a large collection of carts, carriages and ploughs which were donated by the Langlois family.

There can be little doubt that the things we now use daily will give historians of the future an insight into our way of life. Museums today thrive on just that principle and the move towards increasing realism in displays adds to this. What more realistic display can you get than the reproduction of the exact environment? The National Trust of Guernsey would argue that there is none, and their Folk Museum in Saumarez Park makes the argument convincing, providing a superb evocation of the island's old Norman-French way of life.

The museum centres on the courtyard of an old Guernsey farmhouse in Saumarez Park. Entering through the kitchen door the visitor steps back into the early nineteenth century. Not only is the room set out as it would have been over 100 years ago, full of things from that era, but it also has models of people, dressed in clothes of the time, standing in place.

The kitchen is the biggest room in the house and was where all the family dramas took place. A huge fireplace dominates the room and, rather unpleasantly, consumed dried seaweed, dung and furze. A big brass bashin, or preserving pan, stood in it ready to be used in a variety of ways which included cleaning vegetables, blanching food and even bathing small children!

Cooking on the open fire was done by standing kettles or saucepans on an iron tripod or terpid. A brick oven was used for baking, its door placed in a recess about 4ft above a corner of the hearth. Above it a trapdoor leads to the loft where the fuel was stored.

The museum is set in a large and beautiful park which once formed the estate of Saumarez House, now a States old people's home called the Hostel of St John. The house was built in 1721 and passed by marriage to James de Saumarez in 1783.

During the Battle of Flowers, more than 23,000 people cram into the park, but far more than this use the area in the course of a year. It has a playground which is popular with children, a collection of trees and shrubs which are the envy of many gardeners, and flocks of pigeons and ducks that are admired by many. Around the hostel are beautiful formal rose gardens and the arboreal oasis attracts large numbers of migrating birds in season.

The museum shop

THE BATTLE OF FLOWERS

Perry's map ref: p.15 G2
Price guide C (D with seat)
There are special buses
from St Peter Port

This is the single most popular event to take place in the island. Hundreds of people are involved in planning and staging it. Thousands come from all over Guernsey to see it. Some people travel from the other Channel Islands, a few bringing their decorated floats to enter the competition. Faithful fans from the UK and abroad return annually, taking their holidays to coincide with Battle Day, the fourth Thursday of August.

No other event in the Guernsey calendar attracts more attention or people than the Battle of Flowers. More than 23,000 men, women and children crowd into Saumarez Park to watch the skill, artistry and horticultural expertise that goes into each float. These range from the small decorated bikes pushed by children in fancy dress, to huge exhibits more than 40ft long into which blooms from acres of fields are woven. Unlike other festivals of its type held elsewhere, few of the floats for the Battle use paper flowers. Gardens, small allotments and hidden fields all over the island are used to grow a million flowers used in the floats — asters, marigolds, carnations and hydrangeas.

The Battle of Flowers is the highlight of the North Show, the last of four annual agricultural shows (the others are the Royal, South and West Shows). It is a competition, divided into many classes, to see who can design, build and parade the most spectacular float. Voting on the class and overall winners is done by those members of the crowd who buy ringside seats. Visiting troops of scouts collect the votes.

When the competition started a final class was included for the float which held together best as the crowd was allowed to surge forward, pulling the blooms off the netting, and throwing the flowers at each other. It is no longer a feature of today's event, because children and adults were often injured and it was considered too dangerous. Instead, the exhibits are taken from the ground and left in various parts of the island, often to collect money for local charities.

And rightly so, for the floats take months to design. Frames covered in wire take weeks to make and the flowers have to be specially grown. Many people work through the night before the Battle. The blooms are individually wired and then twisted onto the ugly frames, changing them into the fantasies which leave children awestruck, and parents applauding. It was a shame to rip them apart.

FAUXQUETS VALLEY WALK

Perry's map ref: p.14 D5

This walk takes about two hours, has a couple of moderate hills, and includes some of the nicest countryside in Guernsey. It will take you through lanes few people have walked in recent years, past an old waterwheel and into nature reserves run by both the shooting fraternity and National Trust of Guernsey. At times you will forget that Guernsey is an island as long vistas will appear with no sea in them — a rare sight on the island.

Start at King's Mills and turn up past the water treatment works at the bottom of Rue a L'Eau. On your left are the small reservoirs in which much of the silt in the drinking water is trapped, prior to further purification. If you arrive by car this is the place to park.

Walk up the hill past a low wall on your right. This is a culvert for the stream to the water-

works and although it is difficult to see them it has many trout in it. Turn right past a small triangle of grass into a narrow lane, marked as unsuitable for motor vehicles. Within 50 yards you reach a small cluster of buildings which make up Le Moulin de Haut, the site of an old mill. The small ruined building is thought to have been a valet's room detached from the farm.

Proceed up the lane as it enters a stand of trees. Even in the hottest summer this is a cool shady place to walk, often a relief from the crowded beaches. The lane runs on for about a quarter of a mile, meandering slightly and affording lovely views over the valley below. Towards the top of the gentle slope a flooded mill pond is reached. This has recently been taken over and renovated by the Guernsey Society for Shooting and Conservation. They allow no shooting in this area, and as a result it is an oasis for birds, and the plants and insects which often flourish in nature reserves.

Higher up, the lane forks. Take the left turn and follow the road down to the bottom of the valley. For a while you will leave Castel, although if you hold your left hand out over the bank, you will stay in contact with the parish. The boundary with St Andrew's runs along the left-hand side of the road, and is marked by a drinking trough as the stream cuts under the lane.

Called Rue des Fauxquets, the lane rises steeply between deep-cut banks to emerge at the main Candie Road. Turn left and, if you want a short walk, follow the road back down to King's Mills. Otherwise, as the road makes a left bend, turn right into Le Valniquet, a narrow lane which runs down into the Talbot Valley.

After the lane has dropped through a particularly steep section, you will be rewarded with the sight of Guernsey's only working waterwheel. It is fed by the stream which is diverted higher up the valley into a mill race. This finally crosses the lane, via an aquaduct, to drop onto the wheel. A past president of the States Ancient Monuments Committee owns the waterwheel, and restored it beautifully in 1982.

Pass the waterwheel and at the main road, Route des Talbots, turn left. Half a mile down the road, on the right-hand side, is the entrance to a walk which takes you up close to the top of the valley. It has been named Ron Short walk, after a former president of the National Trust of Guernsey which owns the property. It also owns the little cottage, behind which the path rises to give spectacular views before once more dropping to join your route.

The walk makes a pleasant little detour from the main road which continues down to King's Mills. The road passes a field, through which runs the stream that drives the waterwheel higher up the valley. This is one of the most important freshwater wildlife habitats on the island, as it contains a sub-species of dragonfly found only in the Talbot Valley. Fortunately the field is owned by the National Trust of Guernsey and, unless there is some terrible pollution upstream, the unique insect is safe.

Waterwheel in the Talbot Valley

KING'S MILLS

Perry's map ref: p.14 C4

This little village used to be one of the largest settlements on the island, its former name of Les Grands Moullins reflecting its local importance as a centre for milling. Running water is a scarce commodity in Guernsey, but it was the main source of power for centuries. Six mills sprang up in the Talbot and Fauxquets valleys, the largest of which was at the bottom of the escarpment, where the stream lost its power as it flowed out onto the marsh of La Grande Mare.

The waterwheels operated by the stream were driven from above. That is, the water dropped onto the wheel, which turned under the weight

'Wisteria' with its widow's lookout

held in the individual sections. In some parts of the island, the Quanteraine Valley in St Peter's for example, water was brought to the top of the wheel in granite aquaducts. There, and in the Talbot Valley, the stream flowed along the contour line from the mill pond, in an artificial channel or mill race cut into the hillside. This often creates a most peculiar optical illusion, the water appearing to run uphill! The mill race in the Talbot Valley is well preserved and can be seen quite easily from the main road.

King's Mills is unusual in that it was centered on industry rather than the church, although a chapel is thought to have stood at the foot of the hill leading up to La Houguette. The main mill was at the bottom of the Talbot Valley and it was here that the miller would present a sack of corn to La Chevauchee, the colourful medieval cavalcade around Guernsey undertaken by the court of St Michel, ostensibly to inspect the roads.

Many mills were built in the steep valleys during the Middle Ages, when corn was the main crop and flour-based food items made up the staple diet. The mills were either water or wind powered, and most belonged to the seigneur of the fief in which they stood, who charged considerable sums for milling. He thus earned a good income from the corn grown by his peasant tenants. In some fiefs, the seigneur and King were one and the same — this was the case at Les Grands Moullins, hence King's Mills.

You might think this crude form of taxation to be unfair, but the feudal system went even further. The seigneur was the only person who could own a dovecot. This was a ready source of fresh meat, for the birds bred throughout the year. They also fed hungrily through the seasons, usually on the peasants' crops, and thus represented a more subtle form of taxation.

Gentry within the fief might also be allowed to keep a few birds, but not in huge purpose-built dovecots like the ones owned by the seigneur. Their birds would be housed in holes, known as 'volieres a pigeons', in the wall of a barn. One such gable can be seen from the main road at the west end of King's Mills on a barn opposite Orange Lodge.

A description of the whole of King's Mills is outside the scope of this book, but to get a flavour of the area, stand at the junction of the main road through the village with Route de la Hurette, which goes up to St Saviour's Church. This junction marks the division of two military roads, built in the early 1800s. The cottage which forms the corner was in the way of these roads and you will notice that both gables have been trimmed to fit the new road plan!

Opposite the junction is a house named Wisteria, after the creeper which grows over the front of it. In May, before the foliage opens, this bursts into flower with long blue clusters of blossom cascading down the front of the house. On the roof is a widow's look-out, a square balustrade from which the woman of the house would look out across La Grande Mare to sea as she waited for her fisherman husband, or son, to come home. Sometimes she waited in vain. Similar look-outs are to be found in New England and are thought to have been taken there by Guernsey architects who emigrated.

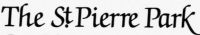

TOMATO CENTRE

Perry's map ref: p.14 B5
Open: summer only,
9.00 - 5.30
Price guide B
Bus routes E1 and E2

Fly over Jersey and you see farms, fields, isolated villages and a few towns. It looks like a piece of the south coast of England that has been ripped off and left in the sea. Guernsey is completely different. Its surface is dotted with greenhouses, many with houses next to them. The practice of covering crops with glass came about because the climate of the island is slightly harder than in Jersey. Cliffs in the south give the face of Guernsey a northern aspect and crops which can be harvested early enough to command good prices in the UK markets cannot be grown in the open.

The first greenhouse on Guernsey is believed to have been built in 1792 by Peter Mourant, who lived in what used to be Candie House, now the Priaulx Library in Candie Gardens. Two of his experimental designs stand against the south wall of the lower gardens, and, built from heavy timbers and small panes of glass, the light intensity inside must be very poor. Heated glasshouses were introduced by W.A. Crousaz, who built several houses using hot water pipes to raise the temperature. They were a great success and by 1887 more than 1,000 tons of grapes were exported annually. The crop gave rise to the name vinery, by which the hothouses are know even today.

Towards the end of the 19th century, the demand for grapes dropped at a time when production increased. At the same time the introduction of steel ships left many Guernsey carpenters unemployed, and they turned their hand to greenhouses, often on their own property, as a second source of income. The crop they concentrated on was the tomato, an exotic fruit first grown as a maincrop in 1884 (although trials had been going on for about ten years). The greenhouses were built like ships, with heavy timbers and small panes, although multi-span roofs and glass sides increased the light intensity inside.

By 1939, the tonnage of tomatoes exported had risen to 35,000 per year — a trade brought to a halt by the Occupation. After the war, the greenhouses evolved further towards today's lightweight, high light-intensity designs.

Some say they evolved too far, for modern greenhouses had become very tall when the fuel crisis hit in the mid 1970s. The growers were faced with huge increases in the cost of heating the wasted space at the top of the houses. The buildings were not as strong either, and storm damage has demolished at least one vinery in recent years.

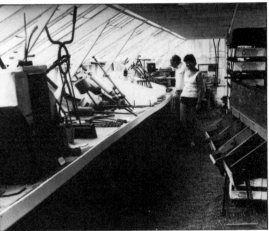
Tomato growing equipment in the museum

Methods of growing tomatoes have changed over the years. Originally they were grown in clay pots; later they were planted in the soil of the greenhouse, and trained up over wires to create the Guernsey arch technique. At the end of each season, the greenhouse soil was sterilised by pumping steam into the rows. Whalehide pots were tried for a while, but today most of the tomatoes are grown in bags of peat which are thrown out at the end of each season.

The irony is that these grow-bags are partly responsible for the decline of the industry — they reduce the possibility of infection from diseases, which in the past got into the soil of domestic greenhouses after a season or two, and made tomato-growing at home a chancy business. Because of grow-bags, many more people can now grow their own, every year.

Bottling tomato wine

A greenhouse is made up of a roof, gables and two side walls known as fronts. In the days when greenhouses were simple lean-tos, the front was a low stone wall on which the roof sat. Vines were planted outside and trained into the house through brick-sized holes in the front. Older houses and lean-tos have many more holes for vines than more recent designs, for the early grape crops were far too overcrowded.

The techniques, and even varieties of tomato grown in Guernsey are best seen in a living museum at the Tomato Centre where a number of greenhouses have been planted using the old techniques. Each is explained by touch-button controlled speakers, video films and cards in the houses. A little gift shop sells souvenirs including the now-famous white Guernsey tomato wine which is made on the premises.

COBO BAY

Perry's map ref: p.8 A4
Open: summer only,
9.00 - 5.00

Prince Charles learned to windsurf in Guernsey while captain of H.M.S. *Bronnington*. In 1976 both he, and the couple who taught him and sold him his first rig, were pioneers. The sport was in its infancy, still rather an eccentric thing to do. Ten years on, events have proved that both Prince Charles and his teachers were setting a trend. He sails his board for pleasure, and the world's press, in many of the places he visits, while his teachers have set up a windsurfing school and shop at Cobo Bay.

With them have come many of the island's beautiful people, both residents and visitors, for although the sport has been taken up by enthusiasts of most ages and both sexes, it attracts a large number of youngsters. They supply the glamour: handsome men crammed into wetsuits, their molls in the briefest of bikinis nonchalantly reclining on decorative beach towels. Fast-moving boards skim across the bay, jump waves and are made to do a wide range of stunts as their skippers swing and duck under the brightly-coloured sails.

Windsurfing can be done by most people of average fitness who are able to swim. Contrary to appearances, it does not require a great deal of strength, and when winds are light it is the most pleasant way to travel along a piece of the coastline, The author has visited tern colonies and watched kingfishers from a board, using the sail as a hide.

Learning the basics takes one or two hours, and the school has training boards mounted on swivelling tripods which stand on the beach. These enable basic balance and technique to be learned without constantly having to climb back on the board from the sea. That comes later and, despite the impression given by television programmes, is quite a short part of the learning process. Soon you become a blithe spirit able to explore parts of Guernsey previously inaccessible. You can lie on your board and gaze into crystal-clear water through a mask, watch birds, explore the bottom of cliffs and coves, or just thrill to the excitement of speeding across the sea with the wind in your face.

In doing these things you will provide a taste of the action and excitement of the sport for the many people who like to take part from the comfort of a deckchair. No windsurfer stays upright all the time, and the sudden movement of the sail which precedes a great splash is eagerly awaited by many.

Cobo is a beautiful beach. It has lovely sand and safe bathing, with a natural windbreak in the form of a good sea wall. At either end children will find rocks to climb and pools to explore, and there are gullies and groynes which provide privacy in what is a busy spot. A large local fishing fleet of small boats moors in the bay during the summer, the huge red reefs of this part of the coast providing shelter from the prevailing westerly winds.

One reef, Grosse Rocque, has a Union Jack flying from a pole on top of it. The flag is replaced annually, a tradition going back at least 50 years. Popular myth has it that the fisherman who started the tradition was a poor sailor. However, he stayed out fishing far longer than his colleagues for his wife was a dragon of a woman and made his life miserable. When she died he hoisted the flag and from then on went to sea only once a year — to replace it!

St Saviour's

The most prominent landmark in this parish is the Reservoir, the island's major water storage site. It is one of the few places where people can fish in fresh water and a popular spot for walking.

The parish is one of the most rural with many farms and smallholdings which support some of the best Guernsey cattle herds. The airport, another major feature, is partly in St Saviour's. The runway actually spans three parishes and holidaymakers arriving in Guernsey can say they have been in St Saviour's, St Andrew's and the Forest before they have even set foot off the plane!

Although one of the largest parishes by area, St Saviour's has one of the smallest coastlines which includes only Perelle and a section of Vazon Bay.

ST APPOLINE'S CHAPEL

Perry's map ref: p.13 E5
Bus routes E1 and E2

Numerous small 'chantry chapels' were founded in Guernsey in the 13th and 14th centuries. Most were poorly built and St Appoline's is the only one still intact.

The chapel builders believed that if they set up a place of worship and employed a priest their souls would be saved. The investment involved was high — both to build the chapel and to employ, house and feed the priest — and only the wealthy could afford the luxury.

One such individual was Nicholas Henry who obtained a licence to found St Appoline's from the Abbey of Mont Saint Michel in 1392. A charter from Richard II dated 20 July 1394 gave Henry permission to provide a living for a chaplain, who was to pray daily for the salvation of Henry and his wife Philippe!

St Appoline's Chapel is quarter of a mile inland from Perelle Bay, and it was originally called Sainte Marie de Perelle. On the vaulted ceiling is a late 14th century fresco of the Last Supper. Following the Reformation the building was used as a byre and store. The chapel was bought by the States in 1873 to protect it but 100 years later it was nearly derelict and an appeal to restore the building for religious purposes was started.

Restoration was completed in 1978 when a new Costwold stone tile roof, York stone paving flags, an altar of Purbeck stone, new pews and stained glass windows were installed.

The chapel was dedicated to St Appoline, the patron saint of dentists, some time prior to 1452. She was martyred at Alexandria in A.D. 249 by having her teeth and jaws broken in such a way that she starved to death. The building has now been rededicated as a place of worship for Christian unity and services are held from time to time.

There is a small lawned area with seats under trees behind the chapel, which is an excellent place to sit out with a picnic or refreshing drink.

RESERVOIR WALK

Perry's map ref: p.21 G1

St Saviour's Reservoir, the island's major water storage site, flooded three valleys and a village when it was built between 1938 and 1947 (with a break during Occupation). This walk crosses the valleys and traces an ancient 'funeral way' which ran from the flooded village to St Saviour's parish church.

The walk will take between an hour and 90 minutes and is about 2½ miles long. You can stop half way round for refreshments at the Ashcroft Hotel, where you will also find the Guernsey Herb Garden, an intriguing and relaxing place to visit.

The walk starts at the car park off the Rue des Choffins at the north-eastern end of the reservoir. Below the dam is the original pumping station which took water from the Rue a L'Or stream. It now pumps the water required from the reservoir to the mains system. Beside it is the old road which ran from Perelle Bay, under the reservoir wall and through the village to St Saviour's Church.

Cross the 300 yard-long dam wall and turn left into the pine trees that line the bank. The path emerges at Rue des Annevilles which follows the contour of the first valley. The lane wanders to a T-junction where you turn left, immediately passing a cattle trough marked with the date of its construction: 1912. The road rises out of the valley at Les Padins where it passes an unmade track leading to the reservoir on your left. As you walk along the lane, the first views of St Saviour's Church open up to your right.

The lane drops into the second flooded valley and passes close to the water at Moulin du Beauvallet, where the old village mill used to be. Take a path marked 'no horses' which runs off to the right. This is the old 'funeral way' along which pall bearers used to carry coffins. On a more pleasant note, villagers would use it as their route to church.

The path follows a stream that feeds the reservoir and is a haven for wildlife. One bird which cannot be missed is the wren, which serenades passers-by with its loud song. Guernsey's mild climate suits this bird — wrens are killed in large numbers by hard winters. The males see the walker as competition and will throw out challenges all along this path. Kingfishers and grey herons can also be seen from time to time in the valley below.

The path rises steadily but gently until it crosses a narrow lane. Then for the last 50 yards of its length it rises sharply, passing a beautiful farmhouse on the side of the valley before emerging at a major road. A left turn will take you back towards the reservoir, while straight across the main road the path continues to St Saviour's Church. A few yards down to the right lies the Ashcroft Hotel.

The hotel will provide a delightful half hour, as the grounds of the hotel have been laid out as a herb garden. In July, when most wild flowers are running to seed, the banks are a riot of colour and perfume — not only from the flowers, but also from the aromatic foliage of the plants. It is a wonder the garden has anything to show as the hotel uses many of the herbs in its kitchen! No herbicides or insecticides are used in the area, and it is alive with bees and butterflies.

The plants are well labelled with details of their cultivation, culinary and medicinal uses. Some specimens are available for purchase in pots and a range of dried herbs is also available. Guided tours of the garden will be conducted by prior arrangement.

The hotel is dominated by St Saviour's Church which makes a pleasant call on the way back. It consists of a nave, north aisle, vestry and side chapel — all rebuilt at various times since the original charter for the church was granted in A.D. 1030. It has a square tower which was used as an observation post by the German forces during the Occupation. They also built long tunnels under the church for use as a huge ammunition store.

A stone menhir, marked with two Christian crosses, stands at the north-east entrance to the churchyard. This is a reminder of the earlier part of the walk, for it was at such stones that the pallbearers changed over as they became tired. The crosses on the stone were supposed to prevent the devil from joining the deceased at the moment the coffin was handed to the new bearers.

The road back to your starting point runs straight downhill, past the church and Mont Variouf School. Pines line the route when you arrive at the third of the flooded valleys, and the road skirts the contour line as it runs around an arm of the reservoir. Follow it up over a small hill and you are soon back at the car park where the walk began.

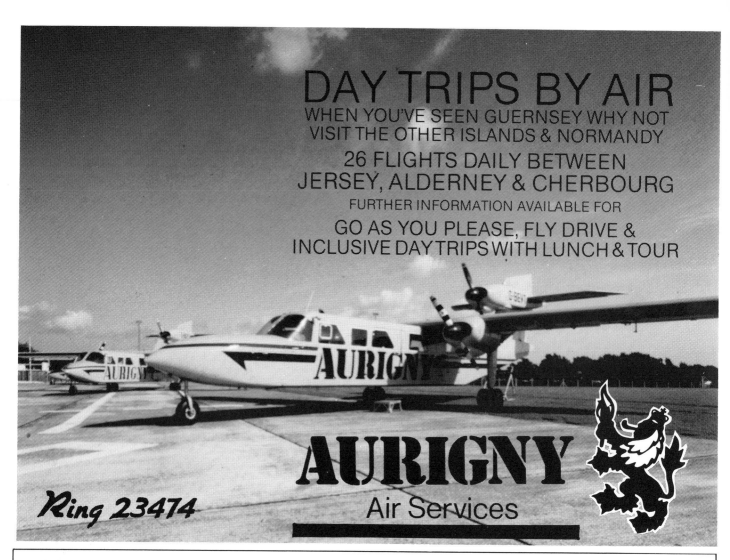

GUERNSEY WOODCARVERS

John Le Messurier carving a coat-of-arms from lime wood

Perry's map ref: p.2 A/B5
Open: every day,
8.00 - 5.30
Price guide: free
Bus routes D1 and D2

Woodcarving and the production of furniture is an ancient craft, but it was not until the discovery of mahogany, imported as ballast in a ship returning from Africa around 1700, that the skill developed into an art. Earlier Tudor pieces, made predominantly of oak, were chunky, thick and heavy, as oak has too coarse a grain for delicate carving. Mahogany allowed craftsmen such as Chippendale and Sheraton to produce the fine delicate pieces which are so prized today.

The woodcarver's skill developed steadily over a long period before another watershed was reached earlier this century when exponents of Art Nouveau, tired of the traditional rules, created a completely new style. Their work, with its bias towards natural shapes and subjects, stimulated the modern woodcarvers whose work is now so popular.

The founder of Guernsey Woodcarvers, John Le Messurier, had the perfect recipe for success — a natural talent and a ready market. He has been 'fiddling with wood' all his life, learning and developing the wonderful skills he draws on. Modern demands for craftsmanship — objects which do not just pop out of the end of a machine — have ensured that he has never been short of work. The business he started now employs a team of nine talented men whose work is in demand all over the world.

The business has two main markets. Besides made-to-order furniture and carvings, the men make 500 or more lines for sale in the showroom as souvenirs and mementos of happy holidays. Many are for use in the kitchen, such as the beech utensils which withstand heat and constant washing. Pastry cutters of various designs are popular, as are rolling pins.

The type of wood used for the work depends on the job in hand. Sycamore is used for bowls, spoons and butter pats as it does not taint the food being served. Ash, another British timber, is used for ornaments when the grain is a feature of the product. The swan platter made in the workshop, for example, relies on the ash grain to give the appearance of feathers. It is a combination of art and functional design, the sides of the plate being carved to form the head and neck of the bird.

More than forty timbers with names such as mukalunga, cedro rana and tulip wood give the workshops an exotic smell. The wood is bought from UK merchants which specialise in decorative, high quality timber imported from all over the world.

Paduk comes from the Andaman Islands, between India and Malaya. Zebra-wood, a member of the pea family, comes from Africa, while the walnut originates from Australia or England. Fruit wood — apple, pear and cherry — is used a great deal as it has a hard close grain. The wood from the 360 species of mahogany is imported from tropical areas all round the globe, but the teak comes from just a few Asian countries.

Besides making furniture John Le Messurier carves sculptures in wood — an art form that uses his skills to the full. The firm also takes pride in the restoration of antiques, a side of the business that requires great knowledge of the materials and techniques of earlier craftsmen.

The finishing touches

63

GUERNSEY GOLD AND SILVERSMITHS

Perry's map ref: p.28 B1
Open: 9.00 - 5.00
Price guide: free
Bus routes D1 and D2

The craft of working gold and silver was probably brought to Guernsey by Protestant Huguenot monks when they sought sanctuary on the island in the 16th century. Following the massacre of the French Protestants on St Bartholomew's day in 1572, large numbers fled from France bringing with them the tools and methods to make fine jewellery, cutlery, plate and religious ornaments.

Bruce Russell

Two silver mines were subsequently established on the Channel Islands to meet the demand for the precious metal. One in Sark employed more than 400 men, brought to the island to work seams which ran from the base of the pit shaft under the sea to the west. It is said that they could hear the boulders rolling above them during gales. That mine went bankrupt, leaving huge debts, while the other in St Martin's, close to the site of Les Douvres Hotel, was banned by parish constables when wells in the area dried up as their water seeped into the mine. Today, silver is bought from London bullion dealers Johnson Matthey and shipped to Guernsey as flat sheets.

Bruce Russell set up and runs his gold and silversmith's business at Le Gron, in a barn which dates back to 1582. He is acknowledged as one of Guersey's leading craftsmen, and is the latest in a long line of Guernsey metalworkers — indeed the hammers he uses have been passed down to him from his grandfather and father.

His business is regularly commissioned to make presentation mementos for visiting VIPs. The wedding present from the people of Guernsey to Prince Charles and Princess Diana

— a silver punch bowl — was made in the workshop. Most of the items on display in the showroom have been made by one of the four craftsmen, who can be watched by visitors as they make the heirlooms and antiques of the future. Demonstrations of the techniques of the craft are given every morning at 10.45, showing how the traditional Guernsey milk cans, two-handled christening cups, jewellery and ornaments are created.

The sheets of gold or silver are cut to size and beaten into rough shapes on the top of an old tree trunk. This wooden block is pitted with a number of hollows, each a different size and depth. Used with a variety of hammers, these govern the appearance of the piece. The tree trunk has been used by three generations of Russells and its use is a fitting start to each item.

The article is next 'raised' or drawn out into shape on a moulded stake. The piece takes its form from the stake and again a range of hammers produce different effects. Raising can be the longest part of the manufacturing process, and it takes many hours to make intricate items such as silver eggs or tankards. The final smooth, precise detail is achieved by tapping the item with yet another type of hammer, flattening all previous marks. This is called planishing, and it has the additional effect of making the metal hard.

Jewellery is also made, and requires minute attention to tiny parts which are sometimes cut and assembled under a magnifying glass. Small chains in gold or silver are the only items which cannot be made on the premises, for these need special machines to make the links. The workshop policy of producing only hand-made goods rules out their production.

Scrap metal from the manufacturing process is returned to the bullion dealers to be melted down. Work involving different metals is kept separate so that the scrap does not become mixed, and even the finest silver and gold sawdust is saved.

Once the piece is complete and hallmarked it is polished ready for display. Polishing is done using a successions of mops, spinning on an electric motor at 3,000 rpm. Each mop is progressively finer and the article sparkles as it approaches showroom quality.

There are two superb showrooms in the complex. The first has the wonderful gold and silver products of the workshop on display while in the second, souvenirs of a more general nature can be bought, along with light refreshments and snacks.

LE TREPIED PASSAGE GRAVE

Situated at the southern point of Perelle Bay, this ancient monument commands a fine view out to sea towards Lihou Island. Access is from Le Catioroc car park, up a path marked with a stone which states 'National Trust of Guernsey'.

A single-chambered tomb, it is about 18ft long, up to 6ft 6in wide and 4ft 4in high. Le Trepied was excavated by Frederick Lukis in 1840, and he found human bones among the artifacts which are now stored in Guernsey Museum. The finds include two barbed-and-tanged arrowheads, and parts of three beakers and two vases. One of Frederick's sons replaced the western capstone, and in 1920 the States of Guernsey reinforced his work by restoring the props which supported the roof. The covering mound is absent, but remains of the entrance passage are just visible.

In a number of 17th century witch trials the tomb was referred to as the midnight haunt of witches, and one of the chief sabbats of Guernsey was held here every Friday night. According to confessions forced from the women, the devil sat on the centre capstone while the witches chanted a mockery of the Virgin Mary as they danced in worship, led by the terrible Heroguiazes. She was said to be Herod's wife — the woman responsible for the order to behead John the Baptist. The tiny summer whirlwinds which ran around the harvest fields were said to be caused by her as 'she shook her petticoats'. Even in the late 19th century no self respecting woman would go anywhere near Le Catioroc on a Friday night.

A few yards to the south of Le Trepied is a cutting into the hillside. This was made by the German forces as part of their coastal railway and is now used by a farmer to store silage.

LA LONGUE PIERRE MENHIR

A mile north of La Trepied, at the side of a (private) drive leading to Fort le Crocq, stands La Longue Pierre menhir, also know as the Witch's Finger. It is a 10ft-high stone (the second largest in Guernsey) and can be seen well from the public road. Lukis dug to the base of the stone, which is incorporated into a field wall, and discovered pieces of grinding stones and pottery on 'an earthen floor'.

Another stone, this one 7ft high and in red granite, stands a few yards away. Re-erected by the States of Guernsey in 1955, this second stone bears resistant areas which resemble breasts — as found on La Gran' Mere at St Martin's Church — and it was possibly selected for this reason.

The whole area is important archaeologically. The field to the north was the site of a destroyed megalithic tomb, again excavated by Lukis, and other standing stones can be seen incorporated into the wall. They probably formed a circle around the tomb. Local experts believe that it was an Iron Age salt working area.

Raising the west capstone of Le Trepied in the 19th century

TORTEVAL

Rocquaine Bay
Portelet Harbour
Pleinmont Point
Route de Pleinmont
Mount Herault
Les Tielles

This is the smallest of the Guernsey parishes with a population of about 943 people. It is the wildest, most remote area of the island and has a considerable area of open countryside. Pleinmont Point, a peninsular which connects the south coast cliffs with the western beaches, dominates the parish and is a major recreation area. Besides the natural attractions such as the birds, flowers and butterflies, the headland is used for motorcycle scrambling, abseiling and clay pigeon shooting.

The parish is cut in two by St Peter's which juts across it, causing some parishioners to leave and re-enter Torteval to get to their church. This can be seen from many parts of the parish and is a good landmark. Designed by John Wilson to replace its medieval predecessor, which fell into ruin in the 18th century, the Anglican church with its steep spire and supporting circular buttress is praised by many and roundly condemned by a few. One of the island's most famous Governors, Sir John Doyle, laid the foundation stone in 1816.

ROCQUAINE BAY

Perry's map ref: p.26 p.32
Price guide: free
Parking: at Pleinmont
Bus routes C1 and C2

The escarpment which stretches from Pleinmont Point past Rocquaine Bay into the parish of St Peter's was once a sea cliff. At the end of the last ice age, the sea level was higher than it is now, and the beaches of today had not formed, for the land was beneath the sea. The boggy strip of grassland which extends down the west coast of Guernsey, and a few raised beaches well above current sea level, show where the old shore line used to run.

When the sea level dropped, the waves eroded this newly-revealed part of Guernsey into new cliffs and beaches — with such success that, towards the end of last century, major works to stop the sea's progress were started by the States of Guernsey. The sea walls along the island's west, north and east coasts, which they began, were eventually completed by the German forces during their occupation of the island in the last war. The walls were originally built in stone, but the job was completed in concrete by the Germans who were masters of construction with this material, as shown by the pillboxes and bunkers which are scattered over the island.

Rocquaine has the highest section of sea wall in the island, reaching 40ft in places. From the bus terminus outside the Imperial Hotel you can see the whole sweep of the wall to the Cup and Saucer. It makes an excellent shelter and the beach is one of the best in Guernsey, although its position away from the big centres of population on the island means that it never becomes packed with people.

A number of boats are moored in the bay and at the neighbouring Portelet Harbour. These small fishing boats belong to both professional and hobby fishermen who take advantage of the good stocks in the area. Pollack, bass and mackerel are prolific in season and are the main fish quarry.

The reefs offshore make fine homes for spider crabs and the large edible crabs, known locally as chancres, as well as crayfish and lobster. Rocquaine Live Shellfish Ponds, over the road from the Imperial Hotel, are a good place to see these creatures. They are kept in saltwater tanks at the ponds to be sold live or cooked on the premises. Light refreshments and a range of cooked seafood is available at the Oyster Bar, and if you fancy a crab salad to take on the beach for lunch this is the place to get it.

Two annual competitions known in Guernesiais as Houlair le Rouleau a Patte and Houlair des Haoutes Bottes — throwing the rolling pin and hurling the welly respectively — are held at Rocquaine. They are just two of the many sea and shore events in the regatta held at the beginning of August each year. A day-long event, starting with shore angling and the local residents' rowing match, it includes swimming and raft races, sailboarding, a long-distance rowing race from St Peter Port to the bay, a parade of decorated boats and powerboat racing. Land events include volleyball and five-a-side football tournaments, a pram race followed by the lawnmower 'grand prix', and a horse and carriage parade.

There is a sandcastle competition, along with a range of events for children which include sack, wheelbarrow and obstacle races, bun bobbing and a treasure hunt. Perhaps the most popular events are the bathing beauty and Mr Rocquaine Regatta competitions which are followed by gurning, the somewhat revolting art of pulling grotesque faces, and piano smashing competitions. The day finishes with a barbecue on the beach, close to the Cup and Saucer. The events are supported by a street market selling a range of home-made foods, bric-a-brac, regatta tee-shirts and the ever-popular Guernsey berets. Crown and Anchor, a local gambling game, operates under licence, and ice-creams and refreshments are available.

The regatta is a modern event, a wonderful day out in what is often regarded as 'the sticks'. The natives are friendly, however, and the day is one of great fun and excitement.

PLEINMONT POINT WALK

Bus routes C1 and C2; start walk from Pleinmont terminus

This ramble will provide an insight into many aspects of island life. You will walk past beaches up which exhausted shipwrecked sailors have crawled, and tread paths first made by slave workers building fortifications during the last war. Ancient Guernsey custom and modern fable are encountered at the start of the walk, and you will have a chance to contemplate the perils of the sea. The walk is about two miles long, will take between an hour and 90 minutes and has one steep hill. It starts at the end of the Rue des Pezeries, Pleinmont, where there is a convenient car park.

Le Table des Pions, Pezeries Point

Le Table des Pions, a large circular group of rocks now known as the Fairy Ring, is the site at which the children of the underworld hold their meetings, according to local guides. The regular dancing of the fairies and elves gives the ring its shape and prevents it from becoming overgrown.

The ring is in fact the place where footmen would eat their lunch during an ancient triennial cavalcade around the King's highways of the island. It is a low dome of turf, surrounded by a circular trench, the outer rim of which is marked with rough stones.

The cavalcade was called the Chevauchee de St Michel, a spectacular and sometimes rowdy affair. Held just before Corpus Christi, the object was to ensure that the roads were clear for processions of the Blessed Sacrament. These were held for periods of a week and were organised by each parish. The court officers of the Fief St Michel would ride around the island's roads attended by one or two footmen, les pions. The route never varied, nor did the stopping places where certain rites of pre-Christian origin were performed. Le Table des Pions was the furthest point the cavalcade reached, and the footmen took a substantial lunch seated at it.

The footmen were bachelors chosen for their good looks. One of the pagan rites observed with gusto by them was the privilege of kissing any young maiden they met. In the early 19th century one lad got hold of the Governor's wife and kissed her with such enthusiasm that the irate Governor banned the cavalcade. It was re-enacted in 1966.

The start of your walk at Pezeries Point, known locally as Land's End, is the most westerly area of Guernsey. It was here that much of the fish catch from Rocquaine Bay was dried.

The name Pezeries is a corruption of the Guernesiaise word epequerie — the ancient feudal right of fish drying — which was carried out in small areas set aside for the job. It seems logical to have them well away from human habitation as the smell must have been very strong.

Until the end of the 19th century the catches, particularly of conger and pollack (known locally as whiting), would be hung out in the perches (areas of about 50 square yards). The technique died out and when the epequeries were no longer used the catch was spread to dry on the thatched roof of each fisherman's cottage.

A well-kept path leads to the top of the steep escarpment, emerging at a T-junction. Turn right, and within a few yards you will reach a car park overlooked by a large German tower. The huge fortification is being renovated by members of the Guernsey Occupation Society, together with a large bunker, the entrance of which is between the tower and the car park.

This is a good place to rest after the steep hill and a convenient seat has been placed on the cliff path a few yards below the ruins of a German lookout post. The view out to sea is dominated by rocks and treacherous reefs off the point, which have been the site of many shipwrecks. The rocks can be seen at high tide, but the danger of the area is most apparent at low water when the reefs which normally hide under the surface appear. During westerly gales many people come out to Pleinmont to watch the sea boiling over them. The sight is most awe-inspiring, and leaves the observer wondering at the sanity of those who go out in boats in such weather — and the bravery of the men who rescue them.

Guernsey's lifeboat has earned one of the best reputations in Britain. A succession of boats and crews have been involved in rescues which have earned them bravery awards. During your exploration of the island the prospect of seeing an event is both slim and unwelcome. However, exercises involving the lifeboat and other emergency services do take place, and these can provide spectacular viewing.

Fortunately, wrecks are few and far between these days, thanks in some degree to the Hanois lighthouse which stands on the worst reef about a mile from shore. The foundation stone was laid on 15 August 1860 and the light first shone out on 8 December 1862. Victor Hugo paid tribute to the lighthouse in *The Toilers of the Sea*, which he wrote while in exile in Guernsey.

The lighthouse was built of Cornish granite, imported together with the masons to build it. The stone was dressed and fitted together on the newly-completed breakwater in St Peter Port, finally being towed to the reef in sections on a barge. The lighthouse is 117ft high and has recently had a helicopter pad built on the top, cutting down the number of occasions when the keepers are stranded by foul weather.

Head eastwards along the Rue du Chemin Le Roi, past the German tower and television masts. These latter relay the BBC radio and television pictures to the island. Their height of 500ft ensures that most areas of the island get good reception.

At the end of the lane, a crossroads is reached. Turn left into the Rue de la Cloture which winds a short way through fields to a T-junction with a breathtaking view over Rocquaine Bay. The white top of the Cup and Saucer, site of Guernsey's maritime museum, can be clearly seen as can Lihou Island when it is cut off at high tide. At low water, the island looks like another west coast headland.

Turn right at the junction and follow Rue du Banquet down the hill for about 100 yards. In a clearing on the left of the road is a path sign-posted to Portelet Harbour. This runs through pine trees, quickly dropping past the beautifully-maintained Trinity Cottages and their gardens, homes of the lighthouse keepers. They have no view of the Hanois, and before the telephone was installed the keepers' wives used to stand on La Varde Rock, a small headland to the west of the cottages, signalling to their loved ones.

The path past the cottages comes out on the main road back to Pezeries Point. Turn left, and within a few yards you reach the slip leading to Portelet Harbour. Slipways were built from dressed granite sets, laid with projecting edges to give horses a good purchase as they hauled heavy loads of vraic, or seaweed, in box-carts up from the beach. There are public conveniences at the top of Portelet slipway and in summer a kiosk provides refreshments.

Head back along the main road, past La Varde rock with its view of the lighthouse, to Fort Pezeries on the headland a few yards from your starting point. Here, during the Napoleonic Wars, guns were mounted to repel the French. A powder magazine was built and can still be seen among the ruins.

Rocquaine Bay, with (inset) an RNLI rescue exercise

Dartford Warblers and Other Birds

Dartford Warbler

Nesting Gannet

The cliff tops which stretch from St Peter Port to Pleinmont Point constitute one large nature reserve with a range of habitats and thus a good variety of birds. Before the introduction of coal to Guernsey, gorse or furze growing on the cliffs was an important source of fuel, and farms all over the island had a piece of cliff land written into the deeds. As their importance diminished, ownership of these strips became confused, and with the exception of a little cutting along the cliff path, the gorse is now largely untouched from year to year. It makes a perfect nesting site for birds.

The most important species nesting in the gorse is the Dartford warbler, a mainly Mediterranean species which is at the very northern part of its range in southern Britain. 'Darties' do not migrate and are killed off by frost and snow during hard winters. Reclamation of their habitats for farming has also hit the species hard in mainland Britain, where they are now rare.

In Guernsey and Alderney they are to be seen in good numbers along the cliffs and with a little patience they can easily be found. They appear almost black at first, skipping across the gorse with their long tails most noticeable. Through binoculars each bird can be seen to have Burgundy-red underparts, a slate-grey back and head, and a prominent red eye.

BAILIWICK OF GUERNSEY
7P
FIRECREST

A Guernsey stamp featuring a firecrest

For thousands of years Guernsey and its neighbouring islands have been stopping-off places for birds on the move. The annual migrations up from the Mediterranean and Africa began at the end of the last ice age. Birds move northwards in spring to make use of the longer day and take advantage of the abundant insect life present in the summer, moving south again when the weather turns cold and the days shorten. Each winter, the islands get large numbers of avian visitors which have been pushed off their feeding grounds by frost and snow, and find a haven in the Bailiwick.

These movements meant that a very wide range of birds can be found in the islands each year. There are few months when migration of some sort does not result in a fresh influx. This can be quite dramatic with vast numbers of arrivals overnight. One winter morning, 250,000 fieldfares were counted on 13 open fields in various parts of the island. During the spring and autumn huge flocks of warblers, flycatchers and finches stop off to feed and drink. The birds can easily be seen as their numbers, and good access to most of the sites, makes observation easy.

Waders can be conveniently studied at high tide from a number of sea-walls along the west coast, by using the walls as arm-rests and hides. The wooded valleys of Petit Bot, Fermain, Fauxquets and the Quanteraine are good areas to watch out for the mouse-like short-toed treecreeper which often associates with flocks of firecrests, goldcrests and titmice.

L'Ancresse is a good site for pipits, larks, chats and occasionally American waders blown across the Atlantic, while its neighbour, the Vale Pond, can produce all sorts of exotic water birds including avocets on occasion. Sea crossings to Herm and Sark will often allow sightings of puffins, razorbills and guillemots. Gannets are frequently seen from these boats, as are shearwaters and skuas. In winter, a large flock of Brent geese takes up residence along Herm's west coast, some coming across to the north-east side of Guernsey.

Guide books to help you identify the birds you might see should always include the birds of Europe, not simply Britain, as the proximity of the continent influences Guernsey birdlife considerably.

Puffin

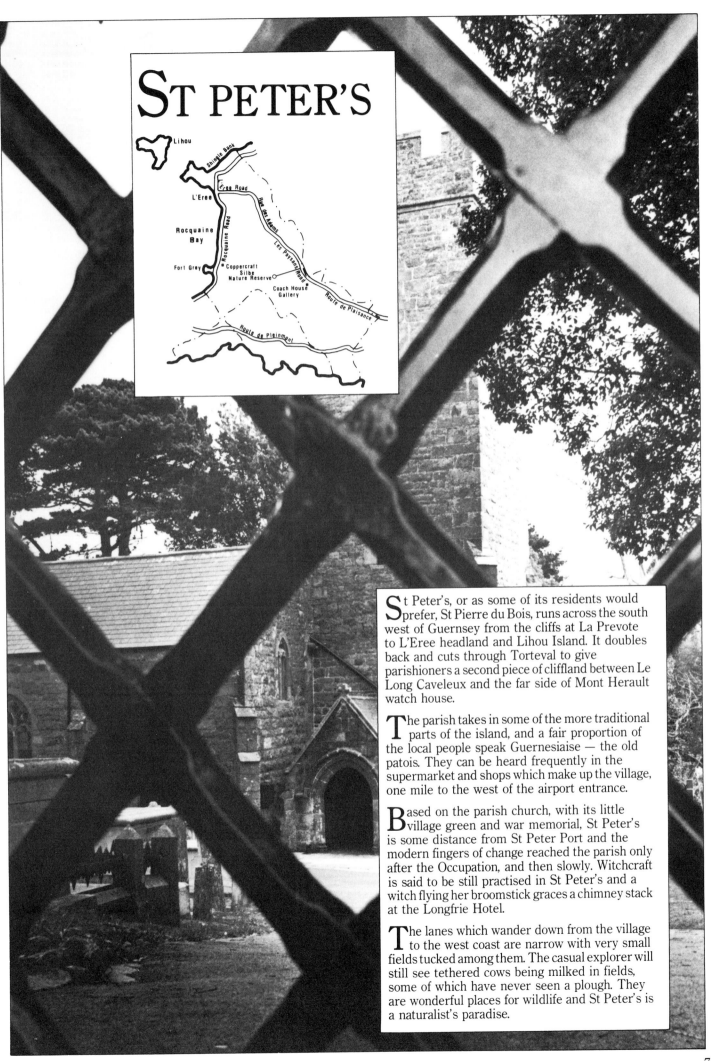

ST PETER'S

St Peter's, or as some of its residents would prefer, St Pierre du Bois, runs across the south west of Guernsey from the cliffs at La Prevote to L'Eree headland and Lihou Island. It doubles back and cuts through Torteval to give parishioners a second piece of cliffland between Le Long Caveleux and the far side of Mont Herault watch house.

The parish takes in some of the more traditional parts of the island, and a fair proportion of the local people speak Guernesiaise — the old patois. They can be heard frequently in the supermarket and shops which make up the village, one mile to the west of the airport entrance.

Based on the parish church, with its little village green and war memorial, St Peter's is some distance from St Peter Port and the modern fingers of change reached the parish only after the Occupation, and then slowly. Witchcraft is said to be still practised in St Peter's and a witch flying her broomstick graces a chimney stack at the Longfrie Hotel.

The lanes which wander down from the village to the west coast are narrow with very small fields tucked among them. The casual explorer will still see tethered cows being milked in fields, some of which have never seen a plough. They are wonderful places for wildlife and St Peter's is a naturalist's paradise.

SILBE NATURE RESERVE

Perry's map ref: p.20 D5
Open: all year round; watch out for bird ringing activities
Price guide: free, but membership of La Societe Guernesiaise is encouraged
Parking: St Peter's Church
Bus routes D1 and D2

This reserve is an excellent example of a west coast valley both in its wildlife and its function. It occupies three fields in the Quanteraine Valley, which has steep sides and a stream running down the middle of it which was used to power a water-wheel at Le Moullin. This stream has a millpond which has been cleared and flooded, which marks the lowest point of the reserve.

The stream originally flowed underground beneath the field above that containing the millpond, protected by a cunningly designed granite culvert, at times 6ft deep. A third field is bounded on one side by the stream and on the other by Rue de Quanteraine which runs down the valley. The upper end of the reserve is marked by an elm hedge, at the edge of this third field, while its side boundaries are the ridges at either side of the valley — the south side is mature woodland mostly of oak, while scrub banks give way to blackthorn on the northern edge.

The Silbe reserve was set up in 1974 when its owner, Mrs Liz Silten, invited the author to ring birds in the valley, and then gave him a free hand to create a nature reserve. Trustees finally established a procedure which allowed La Societe Guernesiaise to own the site and the land was conveyed to them. This established a precedent, and La Societe went on to buy other sites of scientific importance, among them the orchid fields mentioned on page 76.

Nature reserves do not look after themselves, however, and a management committee was set up, under the chairmanship of Mrs Silten and guidance of La Societe's conservation section, to look after the area. They did such a good job that within months the directors of Bucktrout's, the St Peter Port wine and spirit merchants, asked them to run the Colin MaCathie reserve at the Vale Pond. A block of fields on L'Eree Marsh was given to La Societe and ownership of these was partly responsible for the scrapping of plans to drain that area for a golf course. The Silbe nature reserve was thus the seed of Guernsey's conservation tree, and a great debt is owed to Mrs Silten for her foresight.

The reserve has been planted with a variety of trees and is open for anyone to wander through. Dogs are not allowed, however, and the usual restrictions have been placed on shooting, and the picking of wild flowers. At one time baskets of primroses were collected each spring and sent for sale in London, but this has been stopped by the management committee.

A considerable amount of bird ringing is done in the valley and advice should be sought from anyone doing this scientific research about the best way to proceed through the reserve. Local ringers are members of the Channel Islands Ringing Scheme and always pleased to show visitors what they are doing, but their nets and any birds caught in them should never be touched.

Parking in the area is very restricted and the best way to reach the reserve is to park at the village green above St Peter's Church, and walk down. Once you have looked at the reserve, carry on down the valley and walk back to the church through the Vinaires lane.

FORT GREY MARITIME MUSEUM

Perry's map ref: p.20 B2
Open: summer only
10.00 - 12.30; 2.00 - 6.00
Price guide B
Bus routes C1 and C2

Standing on a small islet in the middle of Rocquaine Bay, this 19-century Martello tower was built on the remains of an earlier medieval fort. The old Chateau de Rocquaine may have been completely cut off at high tide but today a causeway connects Fort Grey — or the Cup and Saucer as it is affectionately know — to the main coast road. The causeway doubles as a harbour wall for a number of small boats which, when moored at high tide, give the building one of the most picturesque appearances in the island. The fort's tower was painted white as a seamark for mariners many years ago.

Built in 1804 Fort Grey, like Forts Hommet and Saumarez, is broader in relation to its height than the earlier towers on the island, and much stronger. It was one of a line of coastal defences built to ward off attacks from the French but its military value was recognised as recently as the last war, when it was manned as an anti-aircraft battery by the occupying German forces. However, you may wonder why it was built at all — it is inshore of some of the most terrible reefs in the world and only a madman would consider sailing through them to land an army.

Fort Grey is now run by the States Ancient Monuments Committee as a maritime museum and was opened to the public in 1976, although restoration began in 1970.

Getting into the fort is much easier now than it used to be. Before it was converted into a museum, people had to scale the wall with a ladder, but now a wide flight of steps leads up to an entrance which was knocked through the outer wall. The steps are flanked on the left by a huge eighteenth century anchor, recovered from St Peter Port Harbour, and on the right by the Roustel light beacon which was badly damaged after the MV *Winchester* smashed into it in 1970. A stone-built magazine stands at the foot of the outer wall. Within the wall, on the landward side, a second magazine is sunk below ground to the level of its eaves. On the seaward side is a granite-paved gun platform with openings in the parapet marking the positions of cannon which once faced the offshore reefs. One cannon still does, rescued from the wreck of HMS *Boreas* which foundered on the Hanois reef in 1807, 60 years before the lighthouse was built.

The museum has been made inside the white tower. A thick stone pillar runs up the centre of the tower from ground level, through the first floor to support a gun platform above. Entrance to the first floor is through a low doorway above a flight of granite steps. Access to the lower floor used to be down through a trapdoor in the first floor, until a second entrance was made by German troops, who knocked a hole through at ground level.

Relics of wrecked ships

Details of the island's position in the shipping lanes of the English Channel, the treacherous navigational hazards which litter the west coast, and how the Hanois Lighthouse was built, form a backdrop for the stories of many maritime disasters which have occurred around the shores of Guernsey. These are chronicled in detail with artifacts recovered from the wrecks, sad souvenirs of souls who perished when their ships were trapped between an irresistable force and immovable objects — the sea and Guernsey's granite reefs.

The reefs are not quite immovable, however. After being trapped on one for six weeks, the bulk ore carrier *Elwood Mead*, on her maiden voyage, was dragged off by tugs, taking 20 tons of the reef with her, trapped between the inner and outer hulls!

Not all wrecks are modern, and advanced archaeological techniques have been used to recover artifacts from the seabed around the island. The most recent of these projects is the salvage of a Roman wreck from between the pierheads of St Peter Port Harbour. It is such an important task that marine archaeologist Margaret Rule, who raised the *Mary Rose,* has supervised the project. It is hoped that the wreck will form the basis of a second maritime museum in Castle Cornet.

COACH HOUSE GALLERY

Perry's map ref: p.21 F5
Open: daily 11.00 - 5.30
Price guide: free
Bus routes C1 and C2

The degree of local expertise which emerges in a wide range of subjects never ceases to amaze. Musicians, poets and writers, students of the natural sciences, people who are knowledgeable about an astonishing range of topics, all emerge from the 53,000 inhabitants of Guernsey. The same can be said of art, with painters in a wide range of media, sculptors, illustrators and photographers developing skills normally associated with sponsorship, large cities and training colleges.

The Coach-house Gallery is an example of excellence in its field. It has been widely recognised for the achievements reached by an artists' co-operative whose vision brought a standard equal to any country gallery in the U.K. It is a nice place to be, where one can view a wide range of contemporary art in an atmosphere far removed from the stuffy image of traditional art galleries.

It was founded in 1975 in a coach-house along the Braye du Valle, St Sampson's, but moved to St Peter's in 1980. The old premises provided a name for the gallery, but it is now housed in farm buildings so well converted that they received a commendation from the UK Civic Trust in 1983. The complex includes two main galleries, a shop supplying artists' materials and a potter's studio which is an extension of Les Ruettes Pottery in St Andrew's.

The gallery is owned by three people who have ensured that it is light and airy — a fitting place to see the beautiful paintings, prints and sculptures on display. The trio is made up of resident artists Maria Whinney and Barry Owen Jones and administrator Sheila Lintell. Together they aim to raise the standard of pictures on show in Guernsey, while gaining great enjoyment from their art.

The complex is opposite Les Islets Arsenal, a bleak grey stone building on the right-hand side of the road as you come out of St Peter's shopping centre towards the coast. The arsenal was used to store guns and ammunition for the use of the local militia during the Napoleonic era. The gallery makes the corner with Rue des Vinaires and access is through a narrow entrance on the left of the main Les Paysans Road.

Using the etching press

The main gallery is in two parts: the upper floor, which used to be a hayloft, is devoted to monthly displays which usually feature UK exhibitors, while the ground floor shows work of the resident artists involved in the co-operative. These local artists display prints, made on a large etching-press in an adjacent studio, together with watercolours and acrylics. A number of bronzes by Nenne van Dijk and Martin Knowelden are shown and sometimes the work of other local artists, such as Brenda Munson and Laurel Tucker, is displayed in the lower gallery.

The main season of Coach-house Gallery exhibitions is from Easter to Christmas. Occasionally paintings by local artists are displayed, but this is unusual. The work of sculptor James Butler and water colourist Vivian Pitchforth have been shown, and paintings by Jean Hugo, grandson of Victor. Prints by the young print-makers Susan Jameson, Martin Ware and Michael Chaplin have been exhibited, and as this book went to press, Sir Hugh Casson, then president of the Royal Academy, accepted an invitation to show a collection of his watercolours.

Most of the pictures, sculptures, ceramics, glass and other work on display are for sale. Paintings — and prints made on the premises — of island subjects are particularly popular and a great deal of fun can be had exploring Guernsey while staying in one room! They can be bought with or without a frame and make excellent souvenirs.

Next to the gallery is a potter's workshop where most days Tim Babbe works at his wheel throwing a range of bowls, cups, plates, and vases. All his work is done by hand with clay from the main pottery in St Andrew's, where the pieces are taken to be fired. The items are functional and decorative, and can be bought from Mr Babbe in the workshop.

Across the courtyard is a shop, Framecraft, which sells artists' materials, gifts and picture frames. A small gallery has recently been opened to sell antique paintings. The company offers an excellent framing service with a large range of different mounts to choose from to suit both picture and the place where it is to be hung.

Benefit from Guernsey's Peaceful Environment

We provide comprehensive insurance
cover at rates based on
local conditions, tailored to suit
your individual requirements.

The Islands' Insurance Company Limited

Invicta House, Candie Road, St. Peter Port, Guernsey, C.I. Telephone 0481 – 23612

Coach-house Gallery

LES ISLETS, ST PETER'S
GUERNSEY
Tel 65339

PINTAIL DUCK, WOOD SCULPTURE BY GUY TAPLIN

PAINTINGS, ORIGINAL PRINTS, POTTERY, SCULPTURE

OPEN DAILY INCLUDING SUNDAYS　　　　ADMISSION FREE　　　　PERRY MAP REF 21 F5

L'EREE SHINGLE BANK

Perry's map ref: p.12 B5 and C4
Price guide: free, but membership of La Societe Guernesiaise is encouraged
Parking: L'Eree headland - not on the bank, please
Bus routes E1 and E2

Most people have little good to say for shingle banks. They are difficult to walk over, hard to lie on when sunbathing and appear to be devoid of interest, even for nature enthusiasts. The first two judgements might be correct, but a stroll along the pebbles at Fort Saumarez will certainly prove that shingle banks are far from uninteresting.

Shingle banks occur on coastlines where the tide, wind and currents deposit material rather than cause erosion. They are made up mostly of pebbles eroded by the sea, the largest at the top of the bank and smaller ones further down.

Plant colonisation of the top of shingle banks is rapid once it starts above the tide line with little robin, halberd-leaved orache, sea rocket, and the progenitor of the cabbage, sea kale.

A little higher up the bank, away from the sea, a new group of plants takes over. These form a mat of vegetation which includes bird's-foot trefoil, rest harrow, with its sticky leaves, yellow horned poppy, and yellow vetch, together with two clovers — hare's foot clover and clustered clover.

The mat formed by these holds the shingle together and allows tougher plants such as dock and ragwort to get a roothold further up the bank. They have to compete with kaffir fig which has been introduced to the bank but is not welcomed by local botanists as it threatens to swamp the more delicate plants. One of the great finds for visiting flower enthusiasts is the rare Cornish mallow with its soft downy leaves.

The shingle bank is reasonably stable and can be walked on without damaging the environment. Please remember that stonechats, pipits and larks nest on the landward side and ringed plovers are becoming established on the foreshore, so care must be taken when walking, and dogs should be kept on a lead.

ORCHID FIELDS, RUE DES VICHERIES

Perry's map ref: p.20 C3
Price guide: free, but membership of La Societe Guernesiaise is encouraged
Bus routes C1 and C2

This lane wanders across wet meadows formed behind a similar shingle bank to that at Fort Saumarez. They are traditional water meadows, and are the most delicate and as yet completely unprotected environments in Guernsey — despite the fact that they hold 90 per cent of the British stock of loose-flowered orchid, *Orchis laxiflora*. Some are owned by La Societe Guernesiaise and have been saved from ploughing, but each year a few more fields are 'improved' for agriculture and the orchids lost for ever. Drainage of the area could also affect the plants, and would be very difficult for La Societe to prevent.

The loose-flowered orchid blooms in May and June when many of the fields take a purple sheen from the masses of spikes. These are loosely packed with purple flowers which have a white line on the lower petal. The leaves are unspotted. They are found growing with southern marsh orchids and heath spotted orchids. Ragged robin, meadow buttercup, tufted water forget-me-not and ladies smock can also be seen flowering in the late spring and early summer.

COPPER CRAFT

A craftsman at work on a milk can

Perry's map ref: p.20 B5
Open: summer 9.30 - 5.30
daily; winter 8.30 - 5.00
Mon - Fri
Price guide: free
Bus routes C1 and C2

It is said that the first of the distinctive copper cans used on Guernsey for storing and measuring quantities of milk was brought to the island by Norman monks a few years before the Battle of Hastings. Widely used by country folk since then, they have remained unchanged in their design — which is intended to hold the maximum amount of milk within the minimum of metal. They are roughly spherical and have a cylindrical neck with a tightly-fitting lid. A handle, which is strengthened in the larger cans, is fitted over the most uneven of several seams.

Guernsey cans were often used as buckets by milkmaids in the fields. Farmers churned milk in them, and smaller versions carried farm labourers' and workmen's refreshments for the day. In more recent times large cans were used by milkmen to carry the milk on their rounds. The lids of these large cans hold either one or two pints and were used to measure the required amount.

Today the cans are used mainly as ornaments and souvenirs. They are still made by hand at Copper Craft using the same techniques, materials and tools that have been employed for hundreds of years. Each craftsman has slight variations in his pattern, usually in the ridges of the handles and lids, and can identify his particular design. There are just four coppersmiths left on the island, and because of the low numbers involved they have no formal college classes, but serve as apprentices learning the old ways as their instructors did before them.

Guernsey cans are made three at a time. The number of parts involved depends on the size of each can. Small cans have two panels in each half, and those over six pints capacity have three. The jumbo cans have four panels. They are tinned with soft solder on one side, the flux for the the process being painted on to each panel after it has been heated.

The panels are then shaped, or blocked up — an expression which comes from the tree trunk or block on which they are beaten. It has several hollows on the top, which govern the shape of the panel. The shaping is done entirely by eye, which is why each craftsman tends to produce a distinctive style of can.

Seams are made in the panels, using a swage — a piece of steel with a channel in it which bends the copper to the correct shape. The panels are then joined to make the top and bottom halves. Simply beating the seams is enough to make a watertight joint, but they are also soft-soldered. The two halves are then rounded, using a polished stake as a former while they are beaten. They have to be trimmed to the correct size afterwards, as the hammering stretches the copper.

The seam running around the centre of the can is made on a tool called a jenny; the moment of truth occurs when the coppersmith tries the two halves to see if they fit together. The can's neck is made next, wired in place and soldered. It has no lip, but a lid prevent flies and dust getting in to contaminate the milk.

Once the neck is in place, the two halves of the can are soft-soldered together, ensuring that the best seams on each half are in line. The handle is then attached to the opposite side. The bigger cans have a strengthening tie, or boss, between the handle and the body.

Guernsey cans are not the only thing to be made in the workshop. The two coppersmiths take orders for practically any job that can be made in copper or brass. Street lamps, plaques and bowls are all made on the premises. The showroom is well stocked with souvenirs, although they have not all been made locally.

LIHOU ISLAND

The Venus Pool

Perry's map ref: p.12 top inset
Parking: Lihou headland behind Fort Saumarez
Bus routes E1 and E2

Lihou is sometimes an island and sometimes part of Guernsey — it is connected to Fort Saumarez on the mainland by an ancient, rough-paved causeway which dries out at most low tides. It is a wild island of about 50 acres, half of which are farmed, but as the pasture is poor the farming is far from intense. The ruins of a priory, believed to have been consecrated in 1114 and later a possession of Mont St Michel Abbey, stand along the south coast of Lithou. At the southern end, Lithou tapers away to Lissroy Point where a number of shallow rock pools are found. One presents a mystery as it is called Nun's Bath, but the priory was an all-male order!

Access is on foot only, and is dangerous if any water covers the causeway. The area is almost flat and the sea comes up very quickly with a terrible tide race. Many people have drowned after being swept off their feet, and if the causeway has any water over it, do not cross in either direction.

If you enjoy adventure, romance and find a day of peace and solitude appealing, why not consider being cut off on Lihou? The weather needs to be settled and a period of high spring tides — which occur every two weeks — must be chosen. The technique is to cross as the tide is rising, but before it reaches the causeway.

The island is about half a mile long and has a farmhouse which was rebuilt following the Occupation, after the Germans had used it as target practice for some of their west coast batteries. The farm was rebuilt by the last owner, Colonel Pat Wootton, who bought the Crown lease of the island in 1961. Col. Wootton was an eccentric man whose ideas were never totally accepted in Guernsey. He set up a postal service, printing stamps under permit from the UK Postmaster General to mark the Lihou Youth Fellowship, which ran Christian summer camps. In 1982 he grew tired of running battles with Guernsey's postal, planning and housing authorities, and the Douzaine of St Peter's, and moved to another remote island off the east coast of Canada.

In 1927, one of Col. Wootton's predecessors on Lihou started an iodine factory, obtaining the chemical from seaweed, known locally as vraic, gathered from the shores of the island and other parts of Guernsey. The seaweed was shredded, dried and burned to extract the iodine. The best species for the purpose was coue de vacque, or cow's tail. The iodine trade became so important that South American countries subsidised their own iodine industries to undercut the Lihou business, which finally closed down.

The priory, dedicated to Notre Dame de la Roche, has been excavated several times over the last 200 years. All that can be seen today are several lengths of walling and remains of a vaulted roof which fell in during a severe gale in 1980. At one time it was well furnished with a tiled floor that dated to the 16th century.

Beyond the priory, the island rises to its highest point of about 100ft before dropping down a small but steep cliff to the western seashore. At the bottom of this cliff is a large rock pool some 100ft long, which is a popular spot for swimming.

Further offshore, but accessible on foot at low tide, is a rocky islet called Lihoumel which is a breeding site for seabirds such as shags, herring gulls and great black-backed gulls. Lihou is barren; trees do not grow due to the blast from winter winds, and breeding birds are limited to oyster-catchers, pipits and skylarks.

FOREST

Route de Farras · Route des Landes · German Occupation Museum · New Road · Portelet Bay · Le Gouffre

This parish is dominated by the airport. The runway, however, passes through parts of St Peter's and St Andrew's before passengers disembark in the Forest. Opened in 1939, the airport has been continually enlarged and updated since the war. Like harbours, airports are interesting places — planes of many types may be seen, bringing offshore financiers, tax exiles, politicians, other famous people, and forces personnel, besides the visitors and residents of the island. There is a free public viewing gallery, facing the control tower and main apron of the airport, on the flat roof of the west arrival hall.

A little way down from Le Bourg, just beyond traffic lights on Le Chene hill, is a farm which raises red deer. These beautiful animals are quite tame, and if they are close to the six-foot fencing, good photographs of them can be obtained.

CANDIE MUSEUM

THE STORY OF THE ISLAND
AND ITS PEOPLE · A/V
THEATRE · TEAROOM
OPEN DAILY
SUMMER 10.30-5.30
WINTER 10.30-4.30

FORT GREY

THE HISTORY OF
WEST COAST SHIPWRECKS
IN ROCQUAINE BAY
OPEN DAILY
MAY TO SEPTEMBER
10.30-12.30 & 1.30-5.30

CASTLE CORNET

MILITARY AND MARITIME
MUSEUMS · NOON-DAY GUN
GUIDED TOUR OF CASTLE
OPEN DAILY
APRIL TO OCTOBER
10.30-5.30

Explore the cuisine of The Channel Islands

The islands are famous for their rich variety of restaurants, hotels, inns, wine bars and tea and coffee shops. How do you choose the right place for the right meal at the right price . . . and for the right occasion?
The answers to all these questions and countless others are to be found in

Where to eat in the Channel Islands

Now available — price 90 pence — from all leading bookshops and newsagents in the Channel Islands or direct from the publishers KINGSCLERE PUBLICATIONS LTD., 36 Queens Road, Newbury, Berkshire RG14 7NE. Telephone: 0635 35444

P.S. If you're travelling to the U.K. don't forget that Where to Eat in Hampshire and the New Forest and Where to Eat in Bournemouth, Poole and Dorset are available at Eastleigh and Hurn airports. There are Where to Eat guides for most parts of Britain — Full details from the publishers.

LE GOUFFRE AND LA MOYE MOORING

Perry's map ref: p.28 D5

Le Gouffre has two main attractions — it lies amid some of the most attractive scenery in Guernsey and it is home, in summer, for a fleet of about 15 small fishing boats. There is, as a bonus, a small art gallery where the delicate work of Pamela Dorey is on display, and close to the car park is a licensed cafe which serves bar meals. Dartford warblers may be seen in the gorse alongside the footpath down to La Moye mooring.

The car park is under pine trees at the end of Rue du Gouffre, which leads down from the Mont Marche Estate on Route des Landes, the main road through the Forest. The path to Le Gouffre moorings runs south, out towards the sea; it passes a wooden summer house which was rebuilt recently after its predecessor was demolished by a tree, growing on the bank above, which dropped the wrong way when felled.

The spectacular view in front of you is one of the best in Guernsey. To the right, the cliffs continue to Pleinmont Point, while to the left, the path drops quite steeply down towards La Moye Point which provides shelter for the moorings of a small fleet of fishing boats.

The path continues down the hill until it reaches a wall overlooking the mooring. This is a good place to stop and rest, for the descent is quite steep and the view along the cliffs is spectacular. Les Sommeilleuses is the closest piece of cliffland and masks the entrance to Petit Bot Bay about half a mile away. Across the large bay in front of you is Icart Point with its ever-present cars shining in the distance.

A few yards down this path is a seat, tucked into the gorse on the left, ideal for enjoying the sea view. It will be of more use on the way back, for the climb up from the moorings is steep. Behind the seat is a large bank of gorse which is home each season for a pair of Dartford warblers which can often be seen skipping fast over the top of the thick undergrowth. The dark grey warblers, with their burgundy-coloured breasts, often pop up next to stonechats which perch on the top sprigs of gorse. In spring the male performs a spectacular display flight singing his scratchy song as he flies out and up from the undergrowth. Finally, the bird will throw back his wings in a 'parachute flight', descending to a convenient perch where he will assume the classic Dartford warbler pose with his long tail straight up in the air.

A good path leads down to the right, dropping in a series of steps which are well kept by fishermen and the parochial authorities. After about 200 yards a seat is passed — it too will come in useful on the way up. The land part of the mooring is tiered, with equipment, crab pots, lifebuoys and ropes on each terrace. A winch, which is used to drag the boats up a pair of wooden rails, stands on the top tier. The next is cluttered with crab pots and the third has a corrugated-iron hut which the men use to store their tackle.

The last flat part of the mooring has a handrail to which the boats are tied. You might be forgiven for thinking that a small iron ring, sunk into the rock behind the handrail, was put there for the same purpose, but it was not. Years ago donkeys were used to carry fish and tackle from the mooring to Le Gouffre, and they had to be fastened close to the mooring, but in such a way that their ropes did not tangle with the boats' ties. At one time there were four rings, but only one now survives.

THE GERMAN OCCUPATION MUSEUM

Perry's map ref: p.28 D3
Open: summer only,
9.00 - 5.30
Price guide B
Bus routes C1 and C2

On 30 June 1940 Guernsey was occupied by German military forces, an event which changed the lives of all islanders. No one could anticipate 1945 and the end of the war, and although everyone hoped for the eventual happy outcome, all the information they received from that day on was censored by their new rulers. Meanwhile, families had been split when local schoolchildren were evacuated nine days earlier, 34 people were killed in an air raid, and Hitler's relentless march across western Europe seemed unstoppable.

The kitchen scene

Like the inhabitants of larger countries, Guernsey people had to work out the new rules of life under Nazi occupation. In the years ahead they would face starvation, isolation and a lack of all commodities including clothes and medicine. In some cases even their houses were billeted. They had to decide how far to collaborate with the Germans, what to do about resistance and sabotage, and whether to escape by boat to England, which according to their new masters was due to fall within days.

No Red Cross parcels were received until December 1944 and many new recipes were invented for limpets and snails, seaweed soup, bramble leaf tea and acorn coffee. The Germans obtained great propaganda from their occupation of the Channel Islands. They even prepared a study on how people behaved under Nazi rule so that they could plan the eventual government of the UK.

The full story is told at the German Occupation Museum tucked behind the Forest Church. Founder Richard Heaume was born in Guernsey during the war years and developed the museum in a small cottage from a collection of German artifacts collected after the war. The collection continues to grow, as he is constantly searching for reminders of those black days.

In the entrance hall there is an audio-visual presentation of the Occupation. The walls are hung with wood carvings and paintings by German soldiers, while cabinets along the wall contain instruments from the German Military Band, uniforms and weapons.

The equipment room contains a mass of military equipment, much of it looted by islanders after the liberation. There is printing equipment used by the German press for troops in the island, medical equipment, relics from the Todt Organisation of slaves who built the fortifications, and a large number of field telephones, radios and communications equipment. There is also a large dolls' house, made by an Austrian soldier from Dutch cigar boxes which he probably collected while on leave. Each soldier in the occupying force was given leave every six weeks until D-day, when the nearby European ports were closed.

One of the most famous figures in Guernsey sits at a desk in the corner. He is a life-size model soldier, dressed in German uniform. People all over the world have seen his picture, and for many he is the highlight of a visit to Guernsey.

Hauling the field kitchen out from the tunnel beneath St Saviour's Church

which the war in the English Channel was run. Others, like the ammunition stores next to the Underground Hospital, were used for storage. One such tunnel, running under St Saviour's Church, was explored by Richard Heaume who found some of the stored equipment still in place. He subsequently obtained permission to take out a mobile field kitchen. In 1969 the wall sealing the tunnel was breached, and the field kitchen was brought into the daylight for the first time since the Occupation.

The atmosphere in the tunnel had been so good that the kitchen had deteriorated very little — the remains of the last soup cooked on it still remained in the saucepans! A little rot in the timbers was soon repaired, and the kitchen is now on display at the Occupation Museum. None of the cloth uniforms which were stored in the tunnel had survived, and a large quantity of rubbish such as tin cans was left behind by the excavators. Metal helmets, gas masks, camouflaged capes and rubber dinghies were salvaged, however.

A pair of horses originally pulled the kitchen to the sites where it was used to cook meals for the German soldiers and the slave workers. Gun carriages of similar design which were also used on the island needed a minimum of four horses, but were usually pulled by six. The gun carriages were much heavier than the field kitchen, and had a limber — an ammunition box — slung between the horses and the gun carriage. Three of these special limbers were recovered with the field kitchen.

While this book was being written a new hall was built to mark the liberation of Guernsey 40 years ago, on 9 May 1945. A video film of the liberation can be seen, and there is a reconstruction of a complete wartime cycle shop which serviced the principle mode of transport. The Liberation Hall also has a souvenir shop.

The museum has its own tea room where, although you are surrounded by pictures and drawings of the Occupation, the brew is certainly not made from bramble leaves!

The cottage kitchen is set as it would have looked when curfew fell more than 40 years ago. The time is nine o'clock and a secret crystal set has been brought out of hiding to broadcast the news from London. The Germans often mounted raids for these sets — they were sometimes hidden in saucepans of boiling water, which ruined the set but saved the owner, and according to one local historian, during one raid a woman tucked her set 'in a place no gentleman would search'.

Hitler believed Liberation of the Channel Islands would be the main objective of Churchill and fortified them strongly. This locked up an infantry division, vast amounts of slave labour, and resources which could have been used elsewhere along the Atlantic Wall. In the map and bunker room, there are details of these fortifications, from which few rounds were ever fired except when training. Photographs and maps are on display pointing out the positions of the defences, the minefields and the coastal railway which carried materials to the fortifications.

Some of the artifacts on display have come from the many German tunnels dug under the island, which run underground for miles. Some of these connected gun emplacements with barracks, while others were used as offices from

The tunnel from within

PETIT BOT

Perry's map ref: p.29 F4
Minibus service from
Le Bourg, Forest

The first full-blooded British Commando raid of the Second World War was to have a considerable, though indirect, effect on one of Guernsey's major tourist centres, at Petit Bot. Before the raid, mounted on the coast of Guernsey on the night of 14 July 1940, two hotels stood above the beach. After the excerise, code-named Ambassador, the hotels were demolished by the German forces as they feared that the British might use the buildings in subsequent raids.

The Petit Bot Hotel stood higher than, and to the west of, the Napoleonic tower above the beach, while the Old Mill House Hotel was half way along the shore on the site of the present tea rooms. The foundations of both buildings can be seen today and are still used by holiday makers, albeit for picnics and games.

They were not the first buildings to occupy this beautiful and, even today, remote valley. At least two mills were built in the valley to make use of the water which rushes down the steep gully. The top mill was used to grind corn while the lower one, on the site of the tea room, was used to make paper from old ropes and pieces of clothing.

Access was difficult for the road from Le Bourg had not been built and the track from Le Chene was much as it is today — steep and wet in several places, although well worth the trouble of walking down. This was not the case for smallholders who wanted their grain milling, or for the rope manufacturers, and the mills had ceased to be used by the turn of this century. They, like the hotels, were demolished by the Germans.

Today, access to Petit Bot Bay is from Le Bourg down a steep hill which passes the Manor Hotel, 200 yards from the top. For a time during the Occupation, this was the headquarters of a Luftwaffe fighter unit, equipped with Messerschmitt Bf109 planes. After they left Guernsey, the hotel was kept in readiness for use by German VIPs visiting the island.

After a further 200 yards, a wet area on the left side of the road provides excellent views of birds which use the spot to drink and bathe during the summer. The woods around this area have several pairs of nesting short-toed treecreepers — one of the rare species of birds which attract birdwatchers to Guernsey. They look like little brown woodpeckers as they cling to the bark of trees picking out small insects with their long bills.

A path leads off to the left above this boggy area, following the contour of the hillside before rising to provide a wonderful view down the valley to the beach. Using binoculars, you can look down into the well of the Napoleonic tower which was built around 1780 to protect the island from sea-borne attack over the beach. The path finally skirts the hillside before rejoining the track down from Le Chene.

The main road down the valley, if you choose not to take this detour, drops steeply to the beach. There is a regular minibus service during the summer months — it is worth using, for car parking at the bottom is very limited and always a most frustrating experience. The minibus service connects the beach with Guernsey Zoo on the other side of the airport — a useful distraction for those whose children may become bored with sunbathing on the sheltered beach. The tea rooms have the usual facilities and there is a public telephone kiosk.

The beach is one of the most popular in Guernsey as it is sheltered from all but the most southerly winds and is in the most delightful setting. The top half is largely pebbles but at low tide a large expanse of sand is available. To the left of the bay there are large boulders produced by freezing and thawing during the last ice age which caused the rapid erosion of the valley. The water in the tiny streams would not have had the power to carve out the two great rifts which join half way down Petit Bot. On the right-hand side of the beach is a deep cave popular with children.

Climbing the cliffs is extremely dangerous and should not be tried or encouraged. Many people have died on these cliffs which are sheer at the base, unstable in the middle and topped with impenetrable undergrowth — all factors which make them lethal.

While waiting for refreshments, or for the minibus to take you back up the hill, it is worth watching the only members of the weaver-bird family to breed in Europe. The black-bibbed birds nest in the silver birch trees and their rather untidy, but clearly woven nests are easy to spot. Some nests are the size of a small football and as the adults come in and out you will notice that they are, in fact, house sparrows! They have an abundant food supply from the cafe, but none of their usual nest sites are available, so they revert to the style used before they became dependent on man, and nest in the trees.

St Andrew's

The only landlocked parish on the island, St Andrew's connects the upper parishes with the flat northern parts of the island, and the countryside with St Peter Port. It runs from the airport to the north west corner of town at Footes Lane and has a nine hole golf course within its boundaries. This is part of the St Pierre Park Hotel, although residents there sleep and eat in St Peter Port, as the border between the parishes cuts through the property.

A pub with a macabre name — the Hangman's Inn — now stands on the site of the old gibbet, just outside St Peter Port, at the Bailiff's Cross Road. Below the gruesome inn sign is a stone bearing a cross where it is said Gautier de la Salle received his last communion before he was hanged in 1320 for torturing and murdering Renouf Gautier in Castle Cornet. It is believed that at the time he was Bailiff, but there is no proof of this.

It is more likely, however, that the cross marks the spot where pall bearers were changed as the poor carried their dead to church for burial. People believed that as the coffin was passed from one set of shoulders to the next, the devil could jump in with the deceased, so the change-over took place at specially marked holy places. Such crosses can be seen at various sites all over the island.

LES RUETTES POTTERY

Perry's map ref: p.24 B1
Open: daily 9.00 - 5.30
Price guide: free
Bus routes D1 and D2 to
Bailiff's Cross; walk towards
the Castel Church and
follow the signs after 200
yards

The number of potteries all over the UK has increased considerably in recent years, both reflecting and stimulating interest in the potter's craft. Recognition of the expertise and talent expressed by potters through their work is now widespread. Great skill is needed in the choice of materials used for pots, and for the various glazes which give the articles produced their distinctive colour and texture. A good potter must have more than a working knowledge of geology to understand the effect that certain rocks, when ground to a powder, will have on a particular glaze.

The items created must satisfy the artist within the potter, and for this reason the choice of subjects and the individual shape and design of each line produced in a pottery are constantly changing. They must also be a commercial success, for the sale of his or her product is, in most cases, the potter's main reason for making it. It is also a measure that we can apply to judge a craftman's skill.

Les Ruettes Pottery is a small studio run by three people, one of whom, Tim Babbe, is based in a small workshop at the Coach House Gallery, St Peter's. The studio is in two parts;

an area where the wide range of items made are on show, and a small work area where Amanda Lee, who founded the pottery in 1975, and Paul Dyer make the pots.

The showroom has many small sets of pottery in different colours and textures. Each set reflects not only the skill involved in producing the jugs, vases, bowls and mugs, but also the knowledge of how different designs respond to the heat of the kiln.

As you would expect, the choice of material governs the appearance of the final product. Most items are made from clay mixed in huge batches by an old machine once used for making dough. The recipe is far removed from those used in the bakery: 'Take two hundredweight of ball clay, one each from Devon and Cornwall and mix to a fine tilth. Add one hundredweight of fire clay from Stoke-on-Trent and water — continue mixing to produce a soft paste.'

The paste is very sticky and must be spread, a small quantity at a time, onto asbestos bats to dry. Once at the right consistency it is wedged by hand — an operation very similar to kneading — to remove the air which would otherwise produce bumps, known as bloating, as it expanded during the firing.

The pots are thrown on electrically-driven wheels, and then allowed to dry out completely. Any water left in the clay would explode the piece during the first firing. This is done in an electric kiln to a temperature of 960 degrees centigrade and produces a porous matt finish called biscuit. It is then dipped in a glaze and fired for a second time to 1300 degrees. This completes the process, producing the non-porous, glossy or matt, coloured effect desired.

The final appearance is governed by the choice of glaze. These watery mixes are made by the potters from a wide range of powdered rocks and minerals, and ashes of wood or even grass, mixed with a little clay.

The iron content of the glaze determines what the final colour of the piece will be. Blue granite gives a furry grey and pink flecking to a black base, while ash, depending what has been burned to make it, will produce a greeny colour. Red granite, talcum powder and limestone produce variations on these themes, the higher silicone content glazes giving a shine to the product, while calcium leaves a more matt finish.

The three potters produce items which reflect their different specialities. Amanda learned her craft in France while Paul trained in Harrow and Tim in Australia. This breadth of experience is reflected in the products of the pottery: different styles and techniques are always being tried out and the products have changed constantly over the years.

They include traditionally-shaped items ranging from bowls and casseroles to tea set pieces, vases and jugs. A wide range of less likely products, such as orange juice extractors, egg separators, and cider jars are also made. Small perforated pots for bonsai trees, mustard jars and salt pigs prove popular as do the colanders which can be used to steam food over boiling water. All the pottery produced is ovenproof and can be used in microwave cookery.

GUERNSEY ZOO

Perry's map ref: p.22 D5
Open: summer 10.00 - 6.00;
winter 10.00 - 4.00
Price guide C
Bus routes D1, D2 and N

Zoos have the reputation of being either large and impressive, featuring big animals, or small and twee, catering for children. Guernsey Zoo is neither: it is not large, a fact which reflects the lack of local resources, but it capitalises on its size by featuring smaller animals in pleasant surroundings.

The success of zoos as a means of preserving wild animals is illustrated by the Parma wallabies from Australia, which have been taken off the endangered species list thanks to zoo breeding programmes. More than 30 were born in Guernsey during their first seven years at the zoo.

Small-clawed otters make an attractive display near the entrance to the zoo, and on the day the new cafe was opened they stole the show as they amused the assembled guests. Meercats are also very entertaining animals. Very similar in appearance to mongooses, they have an endearing way of standing on their hind legs to check for danger. This often coincides with the arrival of spectators, who enjoy the performance.

Perhaps the nicest-looking animals at the zoo are a troop of white-lipped tamarins which have the most striking rufous underparts, dark grey backs, long tails and white lips. They breed well at the zoo and have recently had their enclosure refurbished to give them more space.

Small-clawed otter

The oldest llama in captivity?

Displays of large animals in what were poor conditions were stopped when the present director, James Thomas, took over the zoo in 1975. The last remaining large animals are a llama, the oldest in captivity, which is seeing out its days at the zoo, and a pair of Himalayan black bears for which an alternative home is being sought.

The gardens are beautifully kept, as are the 400 animals and birds, of 55 species, on show. None have come directly from the wild — they have been obtained by exchange with other zoos.

Mr Thomas puts education high on his list of aims for the zoo. School parties are encouraged to visit — the zoo has an education officer — and the notices about each animal are clearly set out. A breeding programme for some of the obscure and less glamorous animals has resulted in success with two litters of small hairy armadillos — in 1984, the first to be bred in captivity. They have been chosen for breeding because no other zoo seems interested in armadillos.

The birds on display include a pair of impressive eagle owls which are expected to breed within the next few years. They have huge orange eyes and feather tufts which look like ears, giving them an appealing appearance belied by their massive feathered talons. There are also barn owls at the zoo, which have not only bred but have also attracted a wild pair which nest in the elms above the zoo's birds.

It is fitting that the two-toed sloth should be placed near the gate where weary visitors make their way out. Appropriate because each day they spend up to 22 hours asleep! Sloths have suffered terribly from deforestation in South America — they are so slow in their movements that when their home tree is being felled, they cannot get out of it in time.

The sloths are displayed with other animals in mixed cages — a trend Mr Thomas hopes to extend as it provides more variety for animals and visitors alike. Mixed exhibits are not easy to plan, however. The creatures must not eat each other's meals and they should not disturb one another when sleeping. Most important, they should not view each other as potential food!

Meercat

THE GERMAN MILITARY UNDERGROUND HOSPITAL

The system is much larger than the converted underground barracks which was used as a hospital in Jersey. Conditions inside the tunnels are cold, damp and unpleasant, as water from condensation and from the hillside above drips down the walls throughout the summer. As a result little has survived underground, although two of the wards still have bed-frames and the corroded remains of the cooking and heating system can be seen.

The walls are bare concrete, but the remains of a few German directions and ward names can still be seen. Two parallel tunnels run through the hospital wards. There were five general wards, each capable of sleeping 100 people, although they were only used to take soldiers injured in the fighting in France just after D-Day. After six weeks, the patients were taken to surface hospitals, but by then they were starved of sunshine and as white as sheets.

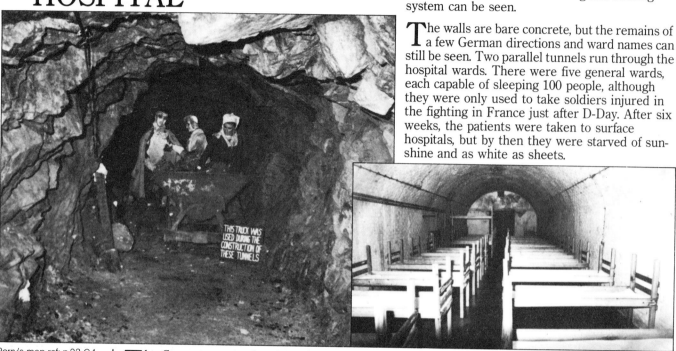

Perry's map ref: p.23 G4
Open: summer only,
9.00 - 5.00
Price guide B
Bus routes D1 and D2

The Germans seemed to have a mole-like desire to build tunnels under Guernsey, and the underground hospital is the largest system built by them during the Occupation. To be accurate, like the other fortifications, it was built by slave labourers from the Todt Organisation, made up of men brought to the island from other occupied countries — France, Spain, North Africa, Belgium, Holland, Poland and Russia — together with a few Guernseymen. They excavated about 60,000 tons of granite, taken out in trucks pushed along rails, and used 15,000 tons of concrete to create more than a mile of corridors and rooms which run under the hillside, in places 75ft deep.

The system of tunnels is in two halves — a hospital which was designed for 500 patients, and a store for thousands of tons of ammunition. The main entrance is in the middle; the hospital area is to the left, while the ammunition store is on the right. Access is through a foyer in which Occupation relics and newspapers are on view. The papers make interesting reading and a copy of one can be bought from the ticket desk. Here a further, rather chilling instruction in given to all visitors: 'Please hand your ticket in when you come out — we want to ensure no-one is lost in there.'

It was not an easy job to dig out the tunnels, and many of the labourers died in the process. Some idea of the hardship is gained as you enter the hospital side of the structure, where one of the old trucks has been placed in an unfinished section of tunnel. The underground chambers had five escape shafts which also provided ventilation, although the system was designed to be resistant to a gas attack. The shafts have rungs built into them and rise between 45ft and 25ft to emerge as square holes in the fields above. Patients could not have been evacuated up them.

The hospital had an operating theatre, X-ray room, mortuary, kitchen, stores, dispensary, staff quarters and a laboratory. It could have taken more patients in an emergency. One of the escape shafts has a reservoir which was filled from a well at the end of the hospital tunnel. It held thousands of gallons of water, making the system independent from outside supplies of any kind.

Ammunition of all sorts was packed into the stores which make up the larger second half of the tunnel system. Based on the same design as the hospital section, it too has parallel tunnels connected by rooms used to store the ammunition. Tarpaulins had to be put over the boxes in order to keep them dry.

The tunnels have a plaque in the entrance which states that they are preserved as a memorial to the Todt slaves who built them.

THE LITTLE CHAPEL

Perry's map ref: p.23 E4/F4
Price guide: free
Bus routes D1 and D2

The healing waters of Lourdes, and the miracle experienced there by Bernadette Soubirous, inspired Brother Deodat Antoine to make the construction of a replica of the Our Lady of Lourdes shrine his life's work. It took three attempts by the unassuming monk to build the tiny grotto known as the Little Chapel, and even then he never saw it completed.

Deodat was a de la Salle monk, of a teaching order known as the Brothers of the Christian Schools, who came to Guernsey from Nantes in December 1913. The wooded slope behind Les Vauxbelets College was ideal for his project, but his first version of the shrine was so small that after some caustic critisism he pulled it down.

The second attempt, built during the First World War, was more successful. It measured nine feet by six and accommodated four people. The Catholic Bishop of Portsmouth visited the shrine in 1923, but unfortunately he was a rather portly man, the entrance was too narrow for him to enter, and he declined to allow the saying of Mass in the chapel. Brother Deodat again knocked down his work.

His third attempt was almost complete when the Second World War broke out, and Deodat returned to France where he died in 1951. The other monks at Les Vauxbelets finished his work, and at the centenary of his birth in 1878 a fund was successfully launched to underpin and restore the chapel.

It is built from clinker, a by-product of the furnaces used to heat the island's greenhouses, and decorated with ormer shells and pieces of china and glass. People from all over the island, and even from abroad, sent broken china and pottery to Les Vauxbelets to be incorporated into what was to become one of the most famous chapels in the world. The entrance, to the left of the building, is marked by two towers and leads into the main chapel. This takes a congregation of about eight people and has a small altar. A flight of steps leads down to a pair of shrines which are so small that during the summer months a one-way-system has to be used for people passing through the building.

GUERNSEY CLOCKMAKERS

At first glance it seems strange to find a clockmaking workshop in a monastery farm building. The need for accurate timepieces was recognised in the 18th century when the prosperity of Guernsey depended on ships' captains, who relied on chronometers for navigation and to calculate the tides. The clocks of the Guernsey clockmakers of that era — Blondel, Naftel and later Paint — are still keeping good time and are now collectors' pieces.

Alas, the art of making the movements has been lost, but the cases in which imported Swiss and German clocks are mounted are still made in this workshop some 50 yards from the Little Chapel. Cases are made from a variety of hardwoods, for barometers and small wall clocks as well as the larger models such as grandfather clocks. Like other craft industries in the island, there are facilities for watching the two cabinet makers at work and some of their magnificent clocks are on sale in a showroom.

This also houses an antique polyphone — an early juke-box. For 10p it will play a tune struck out from a large metal disc inside the mechanism. Polyphones were popular in pubs at the turn of the century, and some were pushed around on barrows and played in the street. Puzzles and games are also available, together with a few novelty clocks. One type relies on a movement which carries ball-bearings around a framework, time being read off from the number of balls in a given section.

Modern and restored clocks tick away gently in the showroom and, surprisingly, it is possible to lose track of time as you contemplate clocks which will be marking the seconds, hours and days for years to come.

Perry's map ref: p.23 E4
Open: daily 8.00 - 5.00
Price Guide: free
Bus routes D1 and D2

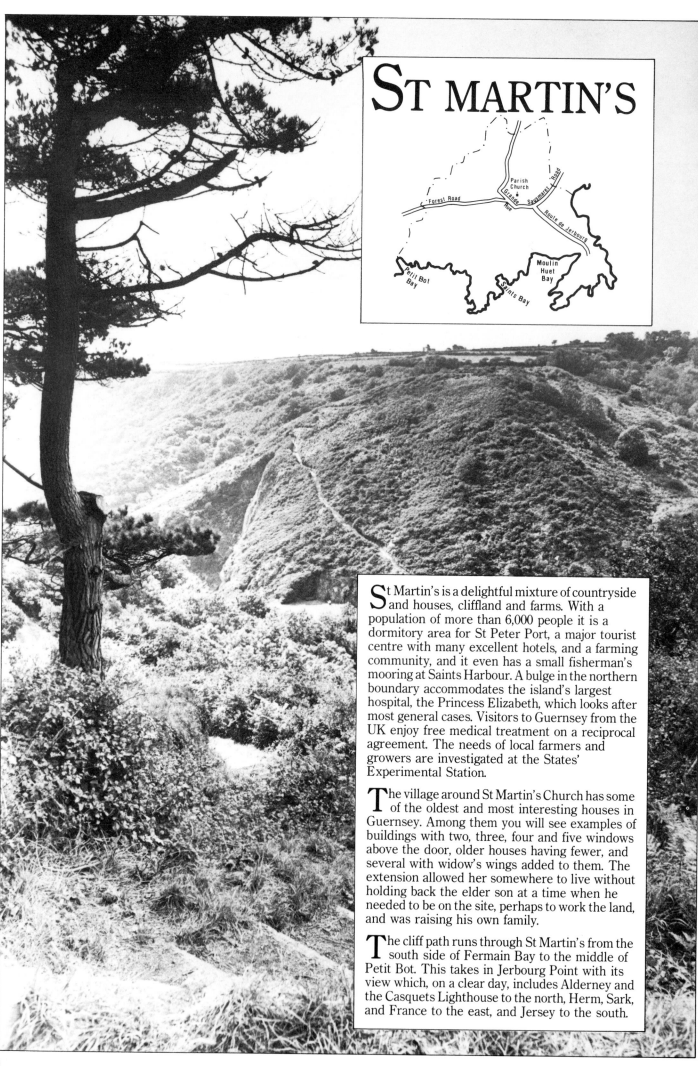

St Martin's

St Martin's is a delightful mixture of countryside and houses, cliffland and farms. With a population of more than 6,000 people it is a dormitory area for St Peter Port, a major tourist centre with many excellent hotels, and a farming community, and it even has a small fisherman's mooring at Saints Harbour. A bulge in the northern boundary accommodates the island's largest hospital, the Princess Elizabeth, which looks after most general cases. Visitors to Guernsey from the UK enjoy free medical treatment on a reciprocal agreement. The needs of local farmers and growers are investigated at the States' Experimental Station.

The village around St Martin's Church has some of the oldest and most interesting houses in Guernsey. Among them you will see examples of buildings with two, three, four and five windows above the door, older houses having fewer, and several with widow's wings added to them. The extension allowed her somewhere to live without holding back the elder son at a time when he needed to be on the site, perhaps to work the land, and was raising his own family.

The cliff path runs through St Martin's from the south side of Fermain Bay to the middle of Petit Bot. This takes in Jerbourg Point with its view which, on a clear day, includes Alderney and the Casquets Lighthouse to the north, Herm, Sark, and France to the east, and Jersey to the south.

ST MARTIN'S CHURCH AND LA GRAN'MERE

Perry's map ref: p.24 C/D5

Christian settlers in Guernsey were no fools. Finding pagan people worshipping all sorts of gods, they built their churches close to, or even on the sites already in use. Two female statue-menhirs have been found within the grounds of churches, at the Castel and St Martin's. The pagan influence of these statues is evident, even today. La Gran'mere du Chimquiere, the grandmother of the cemetery, which stands at the entrance to St Martin's Church, often features in wedding photographs, bearing gifts of flowers or coins. Folklore has it that she will bring fertility to those who treat her so, and there can be no question that St Martin's School is well populated.

La Gran'mere is probably the finest example of a carved menhir in Europe. She stands 5ft 6in. high and is sculptured in some detail. The shoulders, breasts and faintly visible arms were scraped with granite tools by Stone Age people, while much later, perhaps during the time of Christ, her face with its surrounding hair and head-dress was modelled. She was moved to her present position by outraged parishioners who cemented the halves together after she was smashed in two by a pious churchwarden during the last century.

The church replaced an earlier wooden building and probably dates back to the late 12th or early 13th century. It was one of six local parish churches granted to the Abbott of Marmoutier by William Duke of Normandy in 1048, and is named after the founder of that order, St Martin, who was also Bishop of Tours about AD 370.

The porch entrance is the most elegant in Guernsey, built in the decorated style of the English Gothic period (1250 - 1350) which belies the 15th century date of construction. Much of the detail on the stonework has been lost due to weathering, but a sundial at the apex of the roof still tells the congregation whether they are late or not.

The tower and chancel are the oldest-known parts of the church, although some of the stonework in the south and east walls could outdate them. The tower has three bells, recast at the same time as the Town Church peal in 1736, and a rare ringing mechanism which works on the same principle as a barrel organ. The clock dates to 1869, a most significant date in the history of St Martin's Church.

Until then, the parish douzaine had met in the porch, sitting along the stone benches on either side. In 1869 the church was greatly refurbished and the parochial authorities met elsewhere. The font, found in use as a cattle trough at a nearby farm, was returned. It may have been removed for safety when Calvinists came to the island during the Reformation.

New pews were installed at about this time, costing the princely sum of £200. The right to sit in certain pews was attached to ownership of property in the parish, reflecting the responsibility of ratepayers to maintain the church and rectory. The clock was given in the same year by the widow of Frederick de Jersey, a wealthy parishioner, on the understanding that the douzaine would maintain it.

St Martin's Church is fortunate to have the work of one of Guernsey's greatest artists incorporated into the facbric. Miss Mary-Eily de Putron was a maker of stained glass windows with an excellent reputation, particularly in the U.K. The east window of this church was made by her in 1956, using figures of Christ ascended in glory reset from an original given in 1857 to commemorate Captain Richard Charles McCrea of the 64th Regiment, who died at Campore in the Indian Mutiny. Miss de Putron set the figures in tinted glass to make them stand out. She also made the west window in 1957 depicting St Martin together with the arms of England, France and Tours, and the sees of Winchester and Coutances.

The Jacobean style pulpit is an excellent example of oak carving. It was presented in 1657 by the rector, later to become Dean of Guernsey, Jean de Sausmarez. The lectern is also finely carved and is of the same period as the pulpit.

Links with Sausmarez Manor can be seen in the memorials, many of which relate to the de Sausmarez family. The 16th-century Seigneur, George de Sausmarez, died without children and his sister married John Andros in 1543, introducing this famous name to the church. The Carey family are also well represented — comparatively recent residents of St Martin's, they moved from St Peter Port in 1790!

SAUSMAREZ MANOR

Sausmarez Manor is Guernsey's only stately home, but it is not a museum. The house is lived in, and from the start of a visit, there is the feeling that you are having a peep into other peoples' lives.

The gates of Sausmarez Manor tell you immediately that there is something different. They celebrate the return of the de Sausmarez family in 1749 to their ancestral home, after an absence of nearly 200 years during which the house was in the ownership of the Andros family. Mounted on the gate pillars are the family emblems of a greyhound and unicorn, together with two falcons perching on silver helmets. These were sculpted by Sir Henry Cheere, who made many of Westminster Abbey's memorials. There is a legend in St Martin's, encouraged by the present seigneur, that the two animals jump off their pedestals at 12 o'clock on midsummer night and walk, arms linked, down Sausmarez Road!

To the left of the gates is another clue to the house — the courtroom of the fief Sausmarez. This shows that the building is a seigneurie, or manor house. The court meets once a year to note the property changes in the fief.

The house facade is typical of many late 17th-century properties in the states of Virginia and Carolina, USA. Sir Edmund Andros was Governor of New York and Massachusetts, appointed by King William III, and commissioned an American architect to design this house for him. At the time Sir Edmund was also Bailiff and Lieutenant Governor of Guernsey. The low-pitched roof was given an American 'widow's walk' from where the woman could watch out for the

Perry's map ref: p.31 E1
Open: Wed, Thur, Fri;
31 May - 27 Sept.
Train rides and model
railway open: summer
daily 10.00 - 6.00;
winter afternoons Thur,
Sat, Sun.
Price guide: house and
grounds C; train rides A;
models B
Bus route B

When the de Sausmarez family sit down to dinner they are surrounded by ancestors from hundreds of years ago — for if the spirits of their forefathers do not look down on them, portraits do. The walls of the room are covered with portaits, not of nondescript, anonymous people, but of relatives that are as real to the family as any nearest and dearest.

return of her seafaring husband. The dormers have alternate rounded and pointed gables — a design often used in America.

Sir Edmund never saw the house built for he died in London in 1714, leaving his reluctant nephew John Andros to build it. A clause in Sir Edmund's will made sure that this was done, under threat of sanctions! The front, although four storeys high, is only one room thick — behind and attached to it is a Tudor house dated 1585, which replaced the original 13th-century Sausmarez manor.

The house was lost to the de Sausmarez family in 1557 when the seigneur, George de Sausmarez, died without children. He left the estate to his sister Judith, who had married an Englishman called John Andrews. Their son, who became known in Guernsey as John Andros, was declared seigneur in accordance with Guernsey law. Soon afterwards, he built the Tudor house.

Like many islanders in the 16th and 17th centuries, the rest of the de Sausmarez family became wool merchants, with good markets in France. However, the bottom dropped out of the trade when King Louis XIV ordered that nobles should wear silk and satin when attending court in Versailles. Michael de Sausmarez went bankrupt and his son Matthew decided to copy the new French racket of privateering and smuggling, a get-rich-quick way of life. He had no money and married a rich, ugly Jerseywoman, known affectionately as the 'gilded pill' by the present family. Her wealth made up for her looks, and she paid for the first Guernsey fleet of privateers.

Their sons, Philip and Thomas, went into the Navy, starting a tradition which has continued ever since. Both sailed around the world on the *Centurion* under Commodore, later Admiral, Lord Anson. They captured the *Manilla,* a Spanish galleon returning from South America with Inca gold and spices. Philip de Sausmarez was put in command of her, and he sailed the vessel back to London where, at today's prices, her cargo turned out to be worth more than £100m. This made her the richest prize ever captured and Philip's share was a fortune, then, of £5,000. *Centurion's* log of the four-year voyage can be seen in the dining room, under the portrait of Philip.

To commemorate the scoop, George II ordered a competition between four officers of the *Centurion* who were to design a uniform. Philip's won and was adopted as the first naval uniform — a portait hanging in the dining room shows him wearing it. The uniform was changed three years later as the white lapels showed stains from grog and port — always likely to be spilled in high seas. Thomas, Philip's younger brother, can be seen wearing the better-known uniform, with blue lapels, in a portrait also hanging in the dining room.

Philip died in action and left his considerable fortune to his brother John who bought back the fief and house from the Andros family. They sold because Mrs Andros was barren, but no sooner had the sale gone through when she discovered she was pregnant. A son was born and she was so angry that a curse was put on the de Sausmarez family — they would be barren and their 13-century mill would grind no corn. The mill appears cursed to this day, but John's son, Thomas, had 28 children by two wives!

The last major alterations to the house were made by General George de Sausmarez in 1877. He added a large drawing room, the dining room and the entrance porch at which the tour starts. These areas, together with a fine tapestry room which contains the wedding suite of King James II — whose niece Anne Durell was the Jersey 'gilded pill' — and the wainscot room, with its Guernsey-made Chippendale bureau, make up the itinerary.

If you take children around the house, a bribe for good behaviour is the treat of a trip on Guernsey's only train, which pulls carriages on a sightseeing tour around a section of the wooded grounds. There is also an excellent model village and train layout with more than 20 locomotives, 10 working at any one time, in a large Tudor barn. The woodland reserve behind the house has been planted with a wide range of shrubs and plants among the trees.

SAINTS HARBOUR

Perry's map ref: p.30 C5
Parking: difficult — Icart
Point is the closest
Bus route B

Saints is the largest of several harbours along the south coast of Guernsey, and up to 40 boats are moored there at the height of the summer. Access is down Route de Saints from St Martin's, the steep road crossing a cobbled gully which takes a stream across the road rather than under it. A short way above the bay, this road forks. The left fork leads to the beach, where there is a popular tearoom, while the right passes the so-called Martello tower, built between 1780 and 1790. A magazine for ammunition was built some 300 yards away on the hillside above the mooring. It is possible to walk around the tower, but access is barred by a padlocked door.

Most guide books say that the harbour is excellent for swimming, but the author has never been able to find out why. It is a mooring, and as such it is littered with ropes, bits of old netting, nails and store pots, all of which are more than a little off-putting even to keen swimmers. Add to that the risk of being hit by a boat or getting tangled in the ropes and you have a recipe for disaster. As a harbour, of course, there is much to watch, particularly on early summer mornings when the fishermen are putting out to sea.

On the left-hand side of the harbour there is a beautifully made dry-stone slipway leading up to a blocked tunnel. This serves as a boathouse, and contains a winch, used to drag the boats out of the sea. The top of the slip looks like a modern painting as the splashes and spills of paint from boat repairs have stained the stones. Two granite walkways, with handrails to which the boats are tied, run parallel to the side of the bay. Above the mooring is a car park for the use of fishermen.

At the far end of this car park is a large granite pillar in memory of Charles le Febvre, seigneur of Blanchelande from 1854 to 1867, whose contributions helped to pay for the harbour to be built. His fief was at the top of the hill and included the area where the girls' school of Blanchelande College has been built. A harbour wall was almost complete in 1867 when a violent storm swept it away, and the mooring of today was completed in 1906. The granite pillar was thrown over the side of the harbour when the Germans fortified the area, but was recovered and reinstated some time after the war.

A steep cliff path goes up the hill in flights of steps to Icart Point, passing several concrete, rail-mounted gun posts, installed by the Germans who were terrified of attack from the south coast coves.

Saints Bay was the site of a dramatic shipwreck in July 1967 when a small freighter ran aground, straight up the slipway. A courting couple in a car at the top of the slip 'felt the earth move' and, turning on the headlights of the vehicle, saw the name *President Garcia* just visible high up the bow of the ship which had stopped a few feet in front of them!

ST MARTIN'S POINT - SEA FISHING

Most island communities have a strong fishing tradition, and Guernsey is no exception. Naturally, each angler has a few favourite spots which he uses and tends to keep quiet about, but there are many places in Guernsey whose popularity is based on regular good catches. St Martin's Point is among them.

Both red and black bream occur off the point, with the latter being more common. Occasionally, they run in large shoals and big catches can be made using paternoster rigs. The ground around St Martin's Point is rough and tackle has to be quite heavy if bottom fishing is to be tried.

Bass are highly sought-after fish as they are terrific fighters, and good on the table. They are also difficult to catch, although again, if a shoal moves in, look out! Float or ledger rigs will catch them, combined with a variety of baits such as squid, small crabs, lugworm, ragworm and fish strips.

Flatfish such as plaice, sole and flounder are caught in the winter months from a number of sandy bays around the coast, but not St Martin's Point.

If leviathans are your sport, then conger, hauled from the rocks and gullies at night, make an excellent quarry. The baits must be oily so that the fish can make their way up scent streams, and the tackle must be strong with a wire trace to the hook. Night fishing is a dangerous pastime and the usual precautions should be taken. Tell people where and when you will be fishing and stick to those arrangements. Take a friend along with you, and check the spot in daylight to make sure that it is not covered or surrounded by rising tides.

As with many places in southern Britain, the wrasse family are common and will take bait intended for other species. The British rod-caught record for ballan wrasse was set in Guernsey with a fish of 8lb 6oz.

Mackerel start to appear in the late spring and are one of the most common, yet sought-after fish. They often shoal with longnose, or garfish, and the two can be caught on sliding float tackle using sandeel for bait. Experiments have to be made to find the correct depth but then sport can be hectic until the shoal moves off. By setting the float to fish the bait deeper, so that it is close to the bottom, pollack can be caught on the same bait. They like a little movement and so-called float spinning will often catch them where a drifting bait will not.

Other good fishing spots include the lighthouse at the end of the Castle Walk in St Peter Port, and St Sampson's harbour. The moorings at Fermain and Bec de Nez are popular, as are several of the more accessible headlands along the south coast, but paths must be followed down to them — do not climb the cliffs. the flat bays along the west coast are good, especially Vazon, Cobo, Grande Havre, and L'Ancresse. The headlands between them are also popular, and rods can be seen regularly at Fort Doyle, Lihou Island and Pleinmont Point. No permission is needed at any part of the coast, but fishing is banned in parts of St Sampson's Harbour when fuel is being discharged, and at Beaucette Marina. Alderney, Herm and Sark also provide excellent angling.

Bait can either be bought in the Fish Market or found on most beaches, but care should be taken to return rocks moved in the process. Ragworm, lugworm and sandeels can be dug at low tides and crabs are plentiful on rocky shores.

Three angling boats operate out of St Peter Port, and can be joined for half or full day trips. They are often chartered on a daily or weekly basis by groups and clubs. Wreck fishing, on sunken ships up to 30 miles out, is a developing sport, recently made possible by changes in the limitations placed on local angling boats. Records are bound to tumble as the mighty hauls are made. All the boats will provide tackle if asked and bait is included in the price.

FULLY FASHIONED, HAND FINISHED
Traditional Guernseys

The Traditional Guernsey as made by Le Tricoteur is a completely fashioned garment. Le Tricoteur have from the beginning maintained this principle of production because of the considerable advantages it provides in the finished garment. The guernsey is stronger and holds its shape better in both wear and washing because the individual parts are knitted to shape and have selvedges. A further important advantage is that if during rough use a seam bursts, there will be no damage to the garment pieces and it is a simple job to sew up the seam. In the case of a similar accident with a cut-and-sew garment, the individual parts can easily fray and unravel. The necessary repair is at least a major operation and may prove impossible.

MADE IN GUERNSEY, CHANNEL ISLANDS
BY
LE TRICOTEUR
35 COMMERCIAL ARCADE, ST. PETER PORT

CLIFF WALKS

The cliff walks of Guernsey are probably the finest single amenity the island enjoys. They stretch for 16 miles from St Peter Port to Pleinmont Point providing the longest nature reserve, finest views, most varied terrain and a wealth of social history. They have evidence of the German Occupation, Napoleonic Wars, feudal strip grazing and fuel rights enjoyed by nearly every farmhouse in the island.

The first thing that strikes the would-be cliff walker is that the walks are nowhere near as long or as arduous as maps might suggest. Perhaps it is the scenery or the constantly changing point of view that aid the impression that the going is easy. It is at times, but it must also be said that the hills are often steep. However, there are a large number of departure points which lead to main roads with bus services, allowing all but the most infirm walker to do as much, or as little, as he or she wants.

There is the added bonus that many of the beaches along the way have tea rooms and toilets, to say nothing of the most refreshing swimming. Wildlife abounds on the cliffs in the form of countless butterflies in summer, birds in the spring and autumn, green lizards which bask in the sunshine and flowers in bloom during every month of the year.

ST PETER PORT TO JERBOURG POINT

The cliff walk starts at La Valette, St Peter Port, where the path rises up past the Aquarium to Clarence Battery on Les Terres Point. it climbs steadily until Fort George is reached. The fort was built between 1782 and 1812 to cope with almost constant hostilites and tension between Great Britain and France. Clarence Battery was one of its outposts. Fort George housed the garrison until they left in 1940 when it was taken over by the Germans. The fort was destroyed by allied bombers the day before D-day, and it is now an up-market housing estate with a dense population of millionaires, the houses reflecting that wealth.

The path follows the old fort wall until it comes out on La Corniche, aptly named as it follows the cliff top giving wonderful views down through sycamore and elm woodland to Soldiers Bay. The next part of the path is gentle, meandering through the cliffside woodland, past the Germany military cemetery, to the Ozanne Steps which lead down to what was once a private bathing place.

The cliff walk continues until it reaches a confusing maze around Le Becquet Point overlooking Fermain Bay. One path leads down to the moorings, a superb swimming spot which, if not in use, provides good angling. Another path leads up the hill to the Village de Putron, passing the Pepper Pot, or Le Cocquelin, a hollow structure with a ball on top. It was built during the Napoleonic Wars as a sentry box, and is spiral inside. From the centre of the 25ft-high obelisk you can admire views through slit windows and examine the ceiling inside the monument, neatly formed from red brick.

The other paths lead either directly to Fermain Bay or to the road running down to it. The last tower in the series of 15, built around the island between 1780 and 1790, stands overlooking a cafe, sunbathers and a roll-in, roll-out jetty. The ferry from St Peter Port ties up to this landing stage and is worth catching if the walk to Fermain sounds too arduous. As the tide goes out, the jetty is pushed down the beach by some of the brownest men on the island. It is winched up again as the tide comes back in, much to the delight of the small boys who gather on the shingle to watch every summer.

The footpath leaves this activity behind in a long pull up the wooded flank of the valley. A seat at the top makes a good resting place and provides a last look at Fermain Bay. As you take the path signed Bec du Nez, the scenery changes, and you enter the so-called pine woods above La Ricou Point. Of all places in Guernsey, this is the closest in appearance to the Mediterranean, with flat shelves of rock running above the sea and below the trees. It is delightful in winter as well as summer for it will give a good walk in the most severe of westerly gales.

Paths run up the hill at intervals to join the Jerbourg road. Continue along the path signposted to Marble Bay and St Martin's Point and you come eventually to Bec du Nez, a small natural harbour where fishermen land their catches of mackerel, taken off the point, or crabs and lobsters from the gullies under the cliffs. Marble Bay — or Pied du Mur, meaning foot of the wall — is littered with quartz, from which its modern name is derived. The water at this stage looks so tempting that in summer you may decide to stop, take the plunge and cool off.

A gradual slope leads up towards the imposing Idlerocks Hotel before dropping again to run down towards St Martin's Point. Rest at the point for a while — the path up to the German fortifications at Jerbourg is very steep and needs good lungs and legs to make the ascent in one go. At the top you are provided with a much-needed seat and a view to match any in the Channel Islands. On a clear day it is easy to realise that Guernsey is the centre of those islands, for you will see Alderney to the north with Herm and Jethou opposite St Peter Port. Sark is a little further away to the east, and to the south lies that 'other island' of Jersey. On a very clear day the French coast can be made out. There are good toilets at the back of the car park that marks this south-east corner of Guernsey, and a bus and ice cream van stop regularly.

JERBOURG POINT TO ICART

The path from Jerbourg car park goes along a newly-made piece of road, La Moye Lane, for about 200 yards before it reaches a BMX cycle track where it becomes the cliff walk once more. The start of this road is above Telegraph Bay where the telephone cable from Jersey comes ashore. The cliff path runs for a few hundred yards before reaching a standing stone which marks an access track down to a German machine-gun post. This overlooks the Pea Stacks, a remarkable set of rocks made famous by Renoir who painted them from Moulin Huet Beach.

The expanse of water from this point to the next at Icart is known as Moulin Huet Bay, although the cliffs hide the lovely beaches of Petit Bot and Saints Bay. Blanchelande College girl's school can be seen on the cliff top at the far side of the bay. Moulin Huet Valley stretches down to the sea through evergreen oak woodland, and the boats of Saints Harbour brighten the base of the cliff.

The path from this headland leads comfortably northwards until you reach a made-up road leading to the car park above Petit Port. Part of this stretch of cliffland was given to the States in 1959 by the sons of Sir Victor Gosslin Carey, who was Bailiff from 1935 to 1946, and an engraved stone marks the gift.

There are toilets at the car park, reached by passing a German bunker, now used as a fisherman's store. The Germans sliced through parts of the earthworks which stretch from this piece of cliffland, across the main road and down on to the slopes below L'Auberge Divette.

The cliff path continues towards Moulin Huet, but not before giving passers-by the opportunity of descending the flight of steps down to Petit Port Beach. Like all south coast bays the upper shore is made up of rock and pebbles, but at low tide vast expanses of beautiful sand are revealed and the walk down is well worth the effort.

The walk continues along the cliff path, skirting Moulin Huet Hotel and emerging on its access road. The nature of the ramble changes dramatically as the path dives down, past a well and drinking trough, into a comfortable woodland that fills the valley below Le Vallon. It is sheltered, warmer in winter, cool in summer, and teems with birds. The path gets steeper and more narrow as you drop down to emerge at the road leading to tearooms above the Moulin Huet Bay. To your right the road continues up the steep hill to the narrow lanes of St Martin's, but at the bottom of the terraced valley you can rest, get refreshment, and if the tide is high — masking another beautiful beach — dip your feet in the soothing water.

The cliff path sets off up the side of Moulin Huet Valley towards Saints Bay. As it reaches the summit of Bon Port headland, a welcome seat provides a rest with a view back towards Petit Port, the top of which is marked by Jerbourg's Doyle Monument. Built in memory of Sir John Doyle, who as Governor of Guernsey was responsible for the road-building programme and reclamation of the Braye du Valle, it was demolished by the Germans; today's smaller version was rebuilt in 1953.

The cliff path comes out on the road to Saints Bay where, as at Moulin Huet, you can turn right to St Martin's or left down into the valley. This latter choice leaves another to be made, as the road forks left to the beach and right to the moorings. To continue the walk, fork right. Before you reach tower number 14 on the left-hand side of the road, the cliff path branches off up the valley along a gentle rise to Icart. If you decide to drop down to the moorings, there is another path which goes straight up the hillside in steep flights of steps.

Icart headland is worth the climb. Looking back across Moulin Huet and the distance covered gives a sense of achievement, while looking in the other direction towards La Moye Point and Petit Bot Bay gives a taste of things to come. The path skirts a fence — topped with electric wires which turn Les Fougeres d'Icart into a fortress — and rounds the headland to arrive back at Icart car park.

If you want supermarket choice with corner shop service — you'll find it at any of the eight New Island Wide Shops dotted around the Island. We sell everything from mouth watering French Pate to Plastic Buckets and Spades — two of our shops are Post Offices too!

new ISLAND WIDE

We're open 7 days a week and most shops are open from sunrise to sunset.
Here are photographs of all the Shops so that you know what to look for.

Bridge Late Shop - St. Sampsons
Tel. 0481 - 47821
OPEN 7 days a week 8.00am - 9.00pm

Camp du Roi Late Shop - Vale.
Tel: 0481 - 55903
OPEN 7 days a week 8.00am - 9.00pm

Collings Road Late Shop - St. Peter Port
Tel: 0481 - 20561
OPEN 7 days a week 8.00am - 10.00pm

Lyndbrook Late Shop - Les Banques, St. Sampsons
Tel: 0491 - 21630
OPEN 7 days a week 7.30am - 10.30pm

Richmond Late Shop - St. Saviours
Tel: 0481 - 64029
OPEN 7 days a week 8.00am - 9.00pm

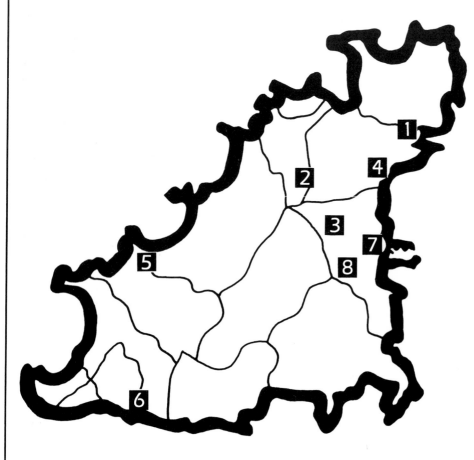

Ville au Roi Late Shop/Post Office - St. Peter Port
Tel: 0481 37733
OPEN 7 days a week 7.30am - 9.00pm

Town Late Shop - Pollet, St. Peter Port
Tel: 0481 - 28402
OPEN 7 days a week 7.30am - 10.30pm

Torteval Shop Post Office - Torteval
Tel: 0841 - 63526 OPEN 8.00am - 8.00pm
Torteval Butchery Mon - Sat 8.00am - 5.30pm
Tel: 65361

ICART POINT TO LE GOUFFRE

Under the pines at Le Gouffre

Perry's map ref: p.25-30
Bus route B to St Martin's
and Icart; minibus in
summer from Petit Bot to
Le Bourg, Forest; bus route
C1 and C2 to the Forest

The cliff path to Icart is better described as a hill path, for the true sheer cliffs have been touched only once at Jerbourg. From Icart through to Pleinmont the walk is along cliff tops between 200ft and 300ft above the sea, with only occasional drops down to beaches and coves. The wooded hillsides and valleys of the east coast and Moulin Huet are exchanged for the gorse, bramble and blackthorn of a typical sea cliff top.

The path is easy compared with the others, staying mostly within 50ft of the same level — quite a relief. For the adventurous, however, it soon reaches the top of a path leading down to Le Jaonnet Bay, named after the gorse thicket it drops through to take you down to the sea. At one time, before the introduction of coal, Guernsey had few trees, and furze (gorse) was the major fuel. Furze breaks, like this one, were cut each autumn and the fuel was collected and stored for the winter in lofts directly above the huge kitchen fires.

Le Jaonnet is one of those places that naturally leads the mind to think of shipwrecks and desert islands, for at low tide yours are likely to be the only footsteps across the beach, and will be clearly visible when you return to the cliff top. Look out for Man Friday's footprints!

It was here that a lifeboat, from which 10 survivors had been snatched earlier, was found in January 1984 after the grain carrier *Radiant Med* foundered 15 miles to the south-west; 19 souls were lost before the Guernsey lifeboat reached the scene to perform one of the bravest rescues in the history of the RNLI.

At low tide you can walk back past the little bay of La Bette towards Icart car park, where under the feet of the cliff walker above, you can explore La Creux au Tchien, or dog cave. Take care to keep an eye on the tide, for it is easy to get cut off.

The cliff path continues towards a stand of pine trees which mark Mont Hubert headland and from which the path drops into Petit Bot Bay. When you reach the pines, glimpses can be caught of an old Guernsey farm, La Falaise, home of composer Robert Farnon, who has written many theme tunes for television programmes. Behind you is one of the most exceptional views in Guernsey, of Petit Bot and La Moye Point. Follow the path down to the tearooms and tower number 13. A minibus service operates from here to Le Bourg, Forest, in summer.

The cliff path rises up to a junction where you can drop down to St Clair battery, which was built at the same time as the tower recently left behind. A few yards futher up the path and another choice of routes is provided. The left-hand path leads down to the little cove of Portelet, which has good sand but is much less populated than Petit Bot.

The right-hand path leads through an enchanting piece of woodland to a road. Turn left and within a few yards you reach Le Variouf hamlet, a little village nestling in a spur of the Petit Bot valley. You can follow the lane up through the village and onwards eventually to Le Gouffre, or retrace your steps to the cliff path. This detour over, the main path leads around a wooded valley, to come out at Les Sommeilleuses — one of the few places in Guernsey where you will hear the 'little-bit-of-bread-and-no-cheeeeese' call of the yellowhammer. The fields behind are used to grow grain crops which attract this lovely yellow bunting to nest.

The path drops down to a wall overlooking La Moye mooring, where on a very low spring tide you can quickly explore the Fontenelle caves below the cliff-top pines. The main path rises up to Le Gouffre valley and the tearoom.

LE GOUFFRE TO LES TIELLES

Prevote Watchtower,
Les Tielles

Perry's map ref: p.27 and
p.29
Bus route C to the airport
and walk down to Le
Gouffre; route C runs along
Route de Pleinmont —
access from Le Bigard, La
Prevote, La Creux Mahie
and Les Tielles

This is where some of the island's rarest butterflies and birds are found. The cliff-top habitat is very special, attracting the year-round presence of Dartford warblers, those dark, Mediterranean birds whose chattering display flight is the highlight of a day's walking for many ornithologists. Masses of butterflies haunt the cliffs, partly because the area has never seen a chemical spray and is rich in wild flowers. The cliff walk is cut by contractors employed by the States Works Department, who have a policy of not using weedkillers, and the whole path benefits as a result.

The walk sets off up the hill to the left of Le Gouffre Restaurant, soon giving views back down the deep gorge. Follow signs pointing to Le Bigard and Pleinmont as your route skirts around the headland, past a rather modern-looking house, to come out on an unmade track. This leads along a shallow but boggy valley, thick with reeds in the summer, to a little hamlet called the Bigard at its head. Take the path once more leading out towards the sea. After taking the rambler under a clump of old pines, it continues for another mile or so to La Corbiere.

Part way along this flat plateau the path dips slightly into a small valley which has a tiny stream running down it. This is a good spot to stop, sit and let the wildlife get used to you. In summer, butterflies will be all around. The rarest to UK visitors is one of the most common in this area — the fast, low-flying Glanville fritillary. This orange-brown butterfly settles on any flower but it is difficult to approach. The only other place it is found in the British Isles is on the Isle of Wight and even in Guernsey it is never seen away from the cliffs.

Other butterflies which will be seen are the common blue, small tortoiseshell and wall brown, which often settles on the path in front of you. A surprise for cliff walkers from the UK will be the frequent sightings of speckled wood butterflies in bright sunshine and open spaces. In the UK they are normally seen in shady woodland glades, but on Guernsey the speckled wood flies out of such places to cavort with other species in the open. A day-flying moth is also likely to be seen — the cream spot tiger moth. This creature has cream blotches on black wings and in flight a brilliant scarlet underwing is revealed.

The butterflies are often to be found on any of the spring flowers still in bloom but sometimes they make their way to a wet part of the valley to drink. There they are likely to be joined by a number of different species of bird, particularly the finches and a pair of Dartford warblers which nest close to the valley.

La Corbiere is marked by a car park from where you can take a short path out towards the sea. There, perched on top of a German bunker, you will enjoy a fine view.

From the car park, the cliff path drops down into a steep valley before rising on the other side. Alternatively, an exciting detour can be made by taking the path down the valley to the strangely named Havre de Bon Repos. Here, instead of finding a harbour with boats enjoying the 'good rest', there is a hostile, rocky beach which would wreck any vessel settling on it. The name must have ironic origins!

A deep pool is left at the eastern end of the beach by the falling tide. It is known as Venus's Pool, and tired walkers can enjoy a swim in water often several degrees warmer than the sea, thanks to its isolation and the effect of the sun. Perhaps it is people who find this area a good place for bon repos.

Back to the cliffs, and up on to the next headland where a large German building marks the site of the Prevote Tower which it replaced. The original tower was built in Napoleonic times as a watch house. The path dips down through the Clifton Valley before following the cliff top, with slight undulations, until it enters another steep valley. On the western side of this valley a path drops down the ridge, taking a steep route to the base of the cliff before bending back to enter the largest cave in Guernsey — Le Creux Mahie.

Once you have returned to the path it is just a short way to the end of this section of the cliffs at Les Tielles. Your approach to the car park is hidden by high stands of blackthorn which have grown up around the remains of a battery and watch tower which once stood on this headland. The car park is 400 yards from the main road, Route de Pleinmont.

LES TIELLES TO PLEINMONT

Perry's map ref: p.26 and
p.32
Bus routes C1 and C2 to
both Les Tielles and
Pleinmont terminus

Guernsey was probably the most heavily-defended territory in Europe once the German occupying forces had built the 14 coastal batteries and 33 anti-aircraft sites which now litter the island. Among them were some huge gun emplacements with a range of more than 30 miles. Peculiar to the Channel Islands were a handful of massive naval direction-finding and signalling stations, similar to the tower built at La Prevote. This section of the walk will take you past several German fortifications, including a large range-finding tower close to the 'top car park' at Pleinmont.

As you leave Mont Herault take a look down into Baie de la Forge where the finest blowhole in the islands sends spouts of water into the air if the tide and wind are right. The next stop along the cliff walk is the German naval range-finder post at L'Angle, from which shipping approaching the Channel during the war was monitored. On the other side of the aptly-named Gull Cliff is another large bunker, often explored by visitors whose island bus tours stop at this car park.

From here, the cliff path wanders between the sea and the BBC relay station's masts, to emerge at a car park above Le Table des Pions. To the right is another range-finding tower. This has been leased by the Channel Islands' Occupation Society who hope to open it to the public when it has been refurbished.

The path sets off from Les Tielles car park, perched at the top of a sheer drop to the sea below. In the spring and early summer, fulmar petrels go through the motions of nesting on the ledges, but although they have done this for a number of years, breeding has never taken place. You might be lucky enough to see ravens drifting effortlessly on the updraught of wind which comes off the sea. These huge members of the crow family nest from early February on a hidden part of the cliff, close to Petit Bot.

The path undulates westwards and although there are a few steep gullies to traverse, the well-kept steps make the going along this stretch fairly easy. In front of you is a rustic-looking stone hut: Mont Herault Watch House, another 19th-century observation post. It is lost from sight as you climb to the Belle Elizabeth headland from where the view back towards Les Tielles includes a cave at Le Long Aveleux.

The view westwards from Mont Herault takes in the whole of Pleinmont plateau, criss-crossed with fields, furze breaks and stands of pine trees. Also visible from the 264ft hill are the German bunkers at L'Angle and at the end of Rue du Chemin le Roi, past the BBC television masts. A road leads from the watch house to Route de Pleinmont — your last chance to leave the walk within easy striking distance of a bus route.

The cliff path follows the contour of Pleinmont headland, with a spur path dropping to the left, zig-zagging down the hill to Le Table des Pions. The top path goes through dense blackthorn thickets and a small pine wood to emerge opposite the entrance to Le Vaux de Monel, a property which belongs to the National Trust of Guernsey.

Rangefinder post at L'Angle

A narrow path drops down through the wild gardens of an old house, now demolished, coming out above Portelet harbour. Turn right and follow the main road past Trinity Cottages, where men from Le Hanois lighthouse have their homes, to a slipway leading to Portelet beach. On low spring tides, commercial oyster, mussel and ormer rearing beds can be seen on the beach. The road passes toilets to end the 16-mile walk from St Peter Port at the bus terminus.

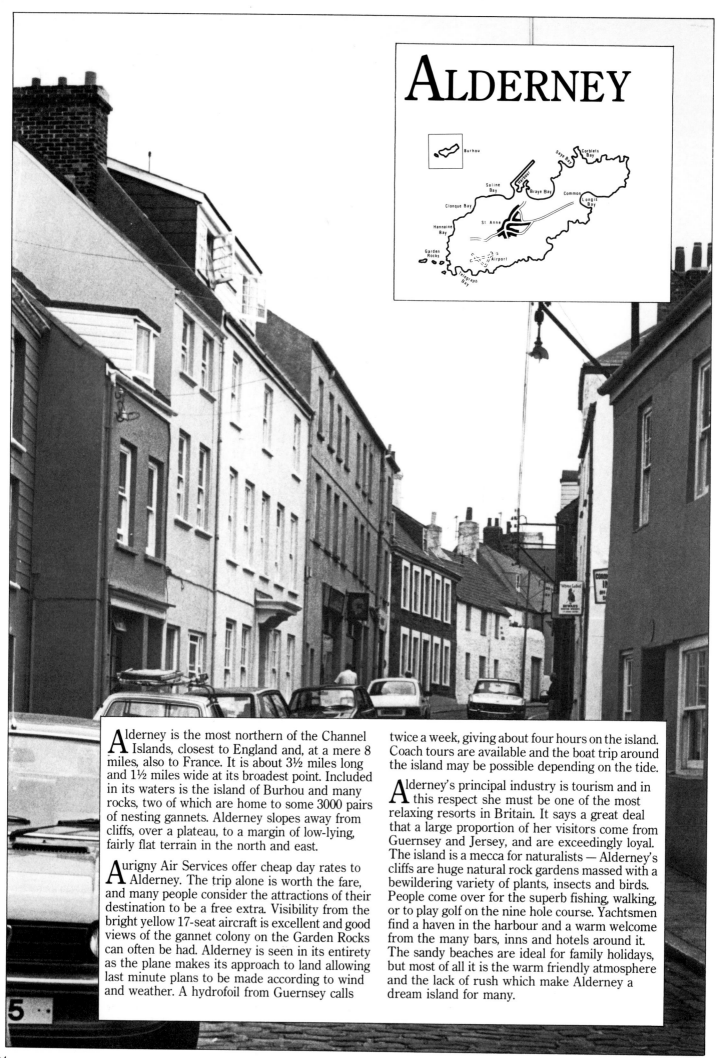

ALDERNEY

Alderney is the most northern of the Channel Islands, closest to England and, at a mere 8 miles, also to France. It is about 3½ miles long and 1½ miles wide at its broadest point. Included in its waters is the island of Burhou and many rocks, two of which are home to some 3000 pairs of nesting gannets. Alderney slopes away from cliffs, over a plateau, to a margin of low-lying, fairly flat terrain in the north and east.

Aurigny Air Services offer cheap day rates to Alderney. The trip alone is worth the fare, and many people consider the attractions of their destination to be a free extra. Visibility from the bright yellow 17-seat aircraft is excellent and good views of the gannet colony on the Garden Rocks can often be had. Alderney is seen in its entirety as the plane makes its approach to land allowing last minute plans to be made according to wind and weather. A hydrofoil from Guernsey calls twice a week, giving about four hours on the island. Coach tours are available and the boat trip around the island may be possible depending on the tide.

Alderney's principal industry is tourism and in this respect she must be one of the most relaxing resorts in Britain. It says a great deal that a large proportion of her visitors come from Guernsey and Jersey, and are exceedingly loyal. The island is a mecca for naturalists — Alderney's cliffs are huge natural rock gardens massed with a bewildering variety of plants, insects and birds. People come over for the superb fishing, walking, or to play golf on the nine hole course. Yachtsmen find a haven in the harbour and a warm welcome from the many bars, inns and hotels around it. The sandy beaches are ideal for family holidays, but most of all it is the warm friendly atmosphere and the lack of rush which make Alderney a dream island for many.

St Anne

Alderney's principal town, St Anne developed high on the hillside above the harbour, possibly as a form of defence against marauding pirates, but more probably to service the fields of the Blaye. These have been farmed in the ancient strip fashion through to modern times so that the farms, with their nucleated communities, have not developed to the same extent on Alderney as they have in Guernsey or parts of the UK. It is in two parts: La Petit Blaye which runs down from the airport, east of the town, and La Grande Blaye which lies to the south.

As you arrive from the airport, 'Town', as St Anne, like St Peter Port, is better known, starts at Le Marais Square, with its beautiful but sadly unused cattle trough in front of the Marais Hotel. The square, like most of the town's streets, is cobbled, and many people say that St Anne has a French atmosphere.

Le Huret leads off the square to the left and runs a short way to a junction. This is at an entrance leading to the museum and, next to it, a clock tower which is all that is left of the old parish church, built in 1763.

Le Huret was the ancient site of the Court of Alderney, which met in the open air. Even today royal proclamations are read out there and a plaque on the wall marks the visit of the Queen in 1957. Follow the main road and you are in the High Street which runs straight out to Longis and the north-east of Alderney.

Turn left and you enter Royal Connaught Square which is dominated, but not over-powered, by the Island Hall — formerly Government House. The area behind the Royal Connaught Hotel is fascinating, with several of the farmhouses which would once have filled St Anne, a pottery close to an ugly German tower, and the red-doored fire station. Roads in this area lead to various parts of the Blaye. On the opposite side of Connaught Square, at the entrance to Church Street, is the old Methodist chapel, built in 1813 and now the Masonic Temple.

The main shopping centre in St Anne runs down the hill along Victoria Street, which joins the High Street close to Le Huret. Victoria Street was renamed after the visit of Queen Victoria in 1854 and achieved importance when the breakwater and forts were built, as it linked the farming side of St Anne with the harbour. The shops of the cobbled street, from which cars are banned in summer, are well mixed with private houses and hotels, and the parish church of St Anne.

Built by Rev. John Le Mesurier, the son of the last hereditary Governor of Alderney, as a memorial to his parents, the church was consecrated in 1850. It is a mixture of both Norman and English styles and is built in both local and white Caen stone. It is large, built to cater for both the local congregation and a garrison — the nave has 18 arches, while behind the apse and high altar is a Lady Chapel. Smaller altars are found in the north and south transepts which form the Memorial and Children's Chapels respectively.

During the war, Alderney's residents were evacuated and the church was used as a store and wine cellar, giving rise to accusations of sacrilege. The bells were carted off and later four were recovered outside Cherbourg on their way to be melted down for munitions, while the other two were found on Alderney. After the war the six bells were recast in the UK and hung when the church was refurbished — a job completed by Christmas 1953.

New Street, a short road which comes off Victoria Street, was renamed after Queen Elizabeth II when she attended a meeting of the States of Alderney in the Court House next to the States Offices in 1978. The court usually sits on Thursdays at 2.30 p.m. but can be visited any time during working hours.

At the bottom of Victoria Street, Les Rocquettes leads up past the Methodist chapel and two hotels to the Buttes. Here, on a hot summer's afternoon, you will hear the click of leather on willow as cricket teams enjoy their sport. Les Rocquettes also leads into Braye Road, a steep hill which links St Anne to Newtown and the harbour. Le Val, a continuation of Braye Road, runs up past the dairy to join High Street. A little lane called Rue des Marcheurs runs down the side of the Methodist chapel into La Vallee, an alternative route to the harbour.

ALDERNEY MUSEUM

Perry's map ref: p.59 G5
Open: Mon-Sat 10.00 - 12.30
Price guide A

The Alderney Society, a body set up to record all aspects of local research, was founded in 1966 and three years later it was given the opportunity to convert the Old School, High Street, into a museum. The Lieutenant-Governor of Guernsey, Sir Charles Mills, opened the building in 1972, since when it has developed into a most interesting museum, finding many ways to preserve and record the island's heritage. In the early 1980s it was realised that the structure of the building was creating conditions far from favourable to the exhibits and a fund was started to raise the £50,000 needed to refurbish the building and add a new wing, which was opened by the Queen Mother in May 1984.

The museum is housed in the main schoolroom and is made up of about 12 sections, each showing a particular aspect of Alderney from its geology through to reflections of the German Occupation. A superb collection of Stone Age flint tools and spearheads indicate the start of man's presence on the island. A 4,000-year-old spear,

found by a visitor in a peat bog, has been preserved and put on display. Early Bronze Age jars and urns fill one cabinet while a succession of finds from close to the Nunnery at Longis make up another display. Boar's tusks are the oldest finds, but the Roman pins, rings, buckle and a superb thimble are probably the most important. Evidence of Roman occupation of the Bailiwick is poor and artifacts like these are helping to piece together details of that era.

The crafts and trades of Alderney are shown, with details of the fishing industry — including a mouthwatering basket of ormers — farming, with dairy tools and butter pats, and a range of artifacts from the lighthouse. The jugs, jars, gadgets and clothing from a Victorian home in Alderney make a fine display.

As with the other islands, the last war left its mark on Alderney. All the people were evacuated to Guernsey and the island became home for thousands of tortured souls from Organisation Todt, slave workers from other occupied countries who were put to work on the defences. Some parts of the island have a strange stillness and atmosphere even today, and troubled thoughts will follow if you dwell on this part of Alderney's past. They will certainly be conjured up when the display of pieces left over from those times is studied. Perhaps the most poignant is a two-tone blue striped shift, worn by some luckless prisoner.

The wildlife of Alderney is illustrated on a number of posters and a charming set-piece of a rope draped over an old hand pump containing two wrens' nests. There are photographs of some of the unfortunate whales which have been washed up on the beaches. These include one, a sei whale, which was kept alive by spraying it with water while waiting for the tide to rise. It eventually went out to sea to join a school of whales which had waited, listening to the grunts, pops and whistles it made while stranded. It is thought that the poor beast became confused when French warships started using sonar a few miles away.

LONGIS COMMON WALK

This walk takes you from the Hammond Memorial on the main coast road out of Newtown, across the common to the Nunnery and up an attractive path to Devereux House, finishing at Fort Essex. The route steers clear of roads and takes you through a range of different scenery.

drag a piece away to make their island bigger. It became stuck before the fishermen could get it home and the resulting island was called Alderney.

The best way across Longis Bay is on the sand, taking shelter, as many sunbathers do, under the concave granite wall. The exit is marked by Alderney's oldest building, the Nunnery. Archaeological evidence, and the herringbone pattern of the stonework, suggests that it originated as a Roman fort, which was probably built as a deterrent to pirates who might have attacked ships moored in the bay.

To get to the Hammond Memorial you can either use public transport, or walk along the Banquage from Newtown, around Braye Bay and up the hill leaving Fort Albert to your left. The memorial is a scallop-shaped area in the fork of the main road to Mannez Quarry. Built in 1966, it has been a place of pilgrimage for many of the Organisation Todt slaves who survived their terrible ordeals in German hands during the war. With the island evacuated of local people, four camps were established to house slave workers imported to build Hitler's fortifications. Many died, to be buried on Longis Common, below the memorial.

Standing facing the memorial, the road forks. The road to the left goes down to Fort Chateau a L'Etoc and Saye Bay. The right-hand fork takes you to one of the most unusual road signs in the Channel Islands — Beware of Level Crossing! The railway from the breakwater to Mannez is used by a train which takes sightseers to the quarry and back. It crosses the road twice within a few yards. At the first crossing, turn right on to a path which leads across the common, stretching away past a reed-bed to the main road as it returns from its circular route around the north of Alderney to Longis Bay. The reed-bed hides La Mare du Roe, and in summer your presence will be greeted by the scratchy song of reed warblers. Turn left at the road and walk to the end of the huge German wall, built to keep tanks off the beach-head above Longis.

A causeway leads from the end of Longis Bay out to Raz island with its fort. The causeway is covered at high tide but makes a fine detour at other times. From Raz, looking to the left of Fort Essex on the hill overlooking the bay, two huge rocks stick out of an otherwise smooth hillside. They are known as the Hanging Rocks, and it is said that ropes were attached to the UK mainland by Guernsey fishermen in an attempt to

Longis is left behind as the road leads up Bluestone Hill, passing Alderney's nine-hole golf course. Rue de Mielles leads back up over the common, past former coastguard cottages to Fort Albert and back to Newtown. Your path comes off the Bluestone Hill road at a turning left up to Fort Essex. Ten yards up the road, a tiny path dives off to the right and follows Barrack Master's Lane up the Val de Fontaine, a popular birdwatching site.

The path reaches civilisation at the Devereux House Hotel where a left turn takes you out to the cliff path. This runs south-west through the most superb scenery to the Giffoine Point, on down the cliff side to Fort Tourgis and Platte Saline Bay, with its gravel works, and on to Newtown. Our walk, however, continues northwards to Fort Essex with its view out across the Race, a treacherous stretch of water between Alderney and the coastline of the Cherbourg Peninsular. The road then drops back down the hill to the Nunnery.

Barrack Master's Lane

Guernsey Post Office START A GUERNSEY COLLECTION

GUERNSEY UNCIRCULATED COINS

Guernsey's coinage features the major industries of the Bailiwick. Collect them in proof sets, in this special pictorial wallet and also look for the £2 commemorative crown.

GUERNSEY MINT STAMPS

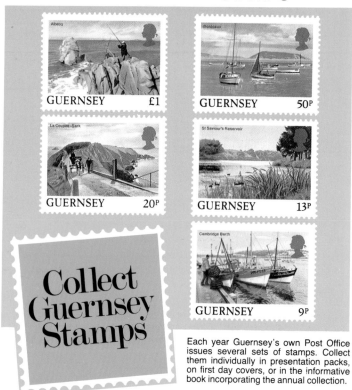

Collect Guernsey Stamps

Each year Guernsey's own Post Office issues several sets of stamps. Collect them individually in presentation packs, on first day covers, or in the informative book incorporating the annual collection.

For further information contact: Guernsey Post Office, Postal Headquarters, Guernsey. Telephone (0481) 26241.

HARBOUR AND BREAKWATER

Swelled by the workforce needed to build the breakwater, the population rose to nearly 5,000. Many were Irish fleeing the famine caused by the failure of the potato crop in 1845. Victoria Street, then called Rue de Grosnez, was lined with new houses and shops while a courthouse and jail were built in the Rue Neuve, today called Queen Elizabeth II Street. A great deal of housing was built elswhere in Newtown and St Anne.

The harbour project stimulated the building of 12 forts in a line, from Fort Clonque, along the north and east coasts to Raz Island. The sheer size of the scheme reflects how much the French were feared. Even the German defences seem minor in comparison, for the forts of Alderney, and the breakwater, must be among the great white elephants of the world. The harbour has been put to military use only once, in 1901, when the Channel Fleet used the anchorage during an exercise.

Alderney harbour pilots were said to be against the building of the breakwater. They believed that it would never stand the onslaught of westerly gales. This may be true, for the breakwater has been extensively repaired after gales, at great cost to the UK Government, since work began in 1847. As big as the breakwater is, during a westerly blow waves crash right over it causing the structure to disappear as water and spray rise high into the air. Pictures of such events hang in several of the bars around the town.

Stone for the breakwater was brought from Mannez Quarry by train and when Queen Victoria and Prince Albert paid a surprise visit in 1857 they landed at the breakwater, and travelled around the island on the train, transferring to a carriage at the quarry.

At the end of the Rue de Braye, opposite the gable of the Seaview Hotel, is the old pier which was built in 1763 to accommodate privateers operated by the Le Mesurier family. This has probably seen far more action, adventure and activity than the breakwater. The lower walkway is called the Douglas Quay, after a former Lieutenant-Governor of Guernsey, Sir James Douglas, who was in office when the foundation stone was laid in 1840.

The breakwater, running north-eastwards from Fort Gronez, dominates the harbour area, and indeed much of that coast, for it can be seen from most high points on Alderney. Built between 1847 and 1864, it was intended to create a counterpart to Portland Harbour on what was to be the 'Gibraltar of the Channel'. The building of a heavily fortified naval base at Cherbourg alarmed the UK Admiralty to such an extent that a plan for two breakwaters and a chain of 12 forts gained approval.

The idea was that a second arm would be built from Roselle Point to create a 67-acre harbour. This plan was later modified — the second arm would run from Chateau a L'Etoc to make a 150-acre pool! Neither were built, leaving the 4,680ft breakwater to stand alone against the elements.

Beyond the old pier is the new jetty which is the main harbour wall, used by all the vessels which call today. The exception is the hydrofoil which has to tie up to a special floating jetty towed in for the purpose. Between the jetty and the breakwater, and in the water beyond, is a safe anchorage for yachts, and in summer the place is crowded with sailing boats.

The harbour is overlooked by a small hill on top of which is the Harbour Office and the Alderney Sailing Club's premises, a popular spot, and first place of call for many yachtsmen when they arrive. A strange wasteland stretches from the hill to Douglas Quay — the site of a huge building which started life housing a stone crusher, was taken over by the Germans and finally demolished in 1972. The road winding past the clubhouse leads to one of the most attractive harbours in the Channel Islands. Surrounded by the bustle of Alderney's fishing industry, it is a quaint and interesting haven, particularly at high tide. Something is always happening on the jetty which runs around the harbour as fishermen tend to their dinghies, repair crab pots and untangle nets, ropes and lines.

The harbour with breakwater in the background

ISLAND TOUR BY BOAT

Skipper: Francis Herival,
telephone Alderney 2375
Price guide G
Trips: summer only, once or
twice a day depending on
the tides and weather

Only a handful of places can offer an island tour as a form of exploration, and those available in the Channel Islands are among the best. In Guernsey, Alderney and Jersey you can get in a coach to see the whole island; in Sark the transport is by pony and cart; in Herm the route has to be followed on foot. Alderney offers another way of exploring her coastline, a tour by boat.

The *Beverley Rose* is clinker-built, and takes 12 passengers and two crew. The 2½-hour coastal tour starts at the breakwater slipway to suit tide times, and the requirements of the people booking. Notices are put up in various parts of St Anne with the details.

The end of the breakwater is given a wide berth as the rocks, tipped into the sea for the foundations, are close to the surface. The boat passes the golden shingle of Platte Saline, with its gravel works machinery standing above the beach. The export of gravel, washed up on this beach by the tides, was a major source of revenue for the island in the past, although demand has declined in recent years.

Fort Tourgis, which marks the start of the path, is passed before setting out for the flat island of Burhou, lying three miles away across a piece of water known as the Swinge. If the weather permits, you can go ashore to get the feel of this island nature reserve. Some areas are out of bounds in the spring and early summer, as they are honeycombed with the underground nests of puffins, and walking on the soft earth can collapse the burrows, trapping the birds.

After a short stop the boat returns to Alderney, arriving close to Fort Clonque, now converted into flats for that holiday-with-a-difference. Visitors staying in the flats can easily find themselves cut off on a high tide, particularly if it coincides with a westerly blow, when great seas roll over the causeway.

The next stop on the boat trip is at the Garden Rocks, opposite Giffoine Point, although no attempt is made to land. Les Etacs, or Garden Rocks, are the home of a colony of gannets which became established during the Second World War, and was discovered by islanders, deported during the German Occupation, on their return to Alderney. The colony was then small, but has gradually increased to about 1,500 pairs spread over two rocks in the group. A similar number nest on Ortac, a stack between Burhou and the Casquets lighthouse. Ortac is also home to nesting kittiwakes, tiny gulls with black tipped wings, and the stack is visited by the boat if a landing is not made on Burhou.

The huge rocks are covered with gannets' nests, each occupied by the handsome birds which will be feeding young, tidying their nests or fighting neighbours. Your boatman and guide, Francis Herivel, will point out the slopes used by roosting birds, and the vast quantities of nylon rope and line built into the nests. This has to be removed occasionally as the gannets get caught

in it and die. Due to the difficulties of landing on the rocks from a boat in the non-breeding season — between November and the end of February — military helicopters have to be brought in. The men take off up to half a ton of nylon! Francis was the first person to land bird ringers on the colonies in the mid 1960s, since which time Alderney's ringed gannets have been found in Senegal, West Africa, Italy, Morocco, Spain, France, Belgium, England and Holland.

The trip continues past Telegraph Bay, where the ruins of a hut can be seen through binoculars. Strands of the telegraph wires, which ran to Guernsey and gave the bay its name, stick out of the hut. The skyline is broken by an old tower which was once a mill. The sand of Telegraph Bay is extensive and golden and may tempt you back when you return to dry land. Take care, however, as the steps down to the beach are cut off at high tide.

A group of rocks called the lovers' chair is passed at Val de l'Emauve. Folklore has it that many years ago the seigneur's daughter, an Alderney maid called Jacquine, and a Guernseyman met at the spot in secret. When they were discovered and attempts were made to stop their affair, the lovers held hands and jumped from the spot into the sea which boils at the base of the cliff. The rock which marked this tragic event was destroyed by the Alderney people, who were afraid others might copy the suicide.

Blue Stone Bay is the next port of call. Some years ago, when the sight of naked people on the beaches was far less common than it is today, naturists took advantage of the bay's seclusion, lying out behind the rocks. An earlier skipper of the *Beverley Rose* would nose her quietly within a few yards of the beach, and give a loud blast on his foghorn. All the sunbathers leaped to their feet to see the cause of this disturbance, diving back behind their rocks like startled seals when they saw the boat and heard the titters and gasps of the passengers.

The tour continues along the south coast of Alderney, beneath the stunning scenery of the cliffs, dipping into coves and examining small colonies of nesting seabirds on the rocks and reefs.

Top: Burhou Island

Above: The 'Beverley Rose'

A ruined pier at Cachaliere is given a wide berth. It looks like a disused scene in a war film — one can almost imagine Japanese fighters dive-bombing the grotesque jetty. It was paid for by the fortune made by an Alderney resident in Chicago, after which city the pier is named, and was used to load granite from a nearby quarry. It became redundant after the steamship *Tyne* foundered on dangerous rocks nearby.

The trip continues past Raz Island, opposite Longis Bay, and on occasions the boat has to fight the tide which rushes through the Race, the stretch of water between Alderney and France. The tone of the engine picks up, but the land seems to move past more slowly as the effect of the tide is felt. The north-east part of the island, marked by the lighthouse at Fort Quesnard, is soon passed and the boat enters the calm waters of Corblets Bay. Saye Bay is crossed and as Bibette Head is rounded, Braye Bay, the break-water and the end of the trip are sighted.

Guernsey Progresses...

...and so does TSB.

— from a simple savings bank to a full service bank.

TSB Channel Islands provides up to date banking and financial services, designed to meet the needs of islanders —

Cheque accounts, deposit and lending facilities, insurance etc — and it's part of the very progressive personal bank, TSB Group.

Banking today with tomorrow in mind.

GIFFOINE POINT

Gannets on the Garden Rocks

The track leading to the south-west tip of Alderney winds around a German gun site before dropping down to the point. As you walk around the emplacement the most astounding sight meets you. The view of a high, white-topped, beehive-shaped rock, with hundreds of large, graceful sea-birds circling over the top, pulls most people up in their tracks. The birds are gannets, and more than 1500 pairs nest on the Garden Rocks. Each has a wing span of 6ft or more and a nine inch long beak which is used to attack any neighbour, or offspring, wandering within range in the colony. At the end of the point, a convenient hollow has suported many pairs of elbows as binoculars are pointed at the birds. The sight is a show-stopper, and indeed has featured on television wildlife programmes.

The Giffoine is surrounded by good places to watch wildlife. Gannets nest above guillemots and razorbills on the stack opposite; fulmar petrels have established a colony on the sheer cliffs beneath the observation point; and across the Swinge lies the bird island of Burhou, with its nesting puffins, storm petrels and gulls. The cliff-path leads away to the left, and in spring you walk though natural wild gardens of bell heather, campion, thrift and bird's foot trefoil; behind is the airport surrounded by the strip cultivation and fields of the Blaye which teem with finches, flycatchers and larks in autumn.

The walk out to the Giffoine from the airport, which is done by many people when they first arrive in Alderney, takes birdwatchers through one of the best sites in the Channel Islands. The fields around the airport are rarely cultivated hard, and weedkillers, insecticides, chemical fertilisers, and intensive monoculture are almost unknown. The hedges and banks abound with migrant birds during the spring and autumn. Gorse patches around the Giffoine are home to whitethroats, Dartford warblers and cuckoos. Hoopoes are a common sight in the spring, the birds occasionally meeting to display their orange crests at each other. Marsh harriers passing through the island often quarter the fields, hunting the rabbits which abound on Alderney. Other birds of prey are seen regularly, and even black kites and goshawks put in an appearance occasionally. Bee-eaters nested once on the south coast some years ago. The Kentish plover also had a toe-hold in the island, but alas no longer nests.

As observers settle down in the gully to study the gannet colonies, inquisitive fulmers drift up the cliffs on their stiff wings, to check out the visitors. They are occasionally joined by one of the ravens which nest below Telegraph Tower, while sparrowhawks, peregrines and merlins all swoop around the cliffs during the migration. A walk towards Hannaine Bay, between the cliff and Fort Clonque, will often be rewarded by good sightings of the puffins which sit on the water, forming little rafts before flying into their rabbit-burrow nest sites on the headland.

Flocks of linnets can be seen flying out to Burhou, but they have to return, for although Burhou has plenty of suitable food plants, there is no standing water, and the birds must drink after eating the dry seeds. Burhou supports many pairs of herring gulls and lesser black-backed gulls, which nest on the ground, often in waist-high bracken. In the early 1950s there were probably 100,000 puffins nesting on Burhou, but the colony has now dropped to about 250 pairs. The decline cannot be accounted for, but it is often blamed partly on great black-backed gulls, and also on increased oil pollution of the English Channel. Rock pipits and shags nest on the granite outcrops which form the spine of Burhou and storm petrels use a demolished wall in which to breed. Their numbers have also dropped in recent years.

The ground around Giffoine Point is carpeted with clumps of thrift and beautiful, yellow-flowered prostrate broom. This is so well adapted to the habitat that it never grows higher than a few inches — a protection against the winter wind. However, it has no defence against greater broomrape, a parasite which draws nourishment from the broom plant. In the autumn the thick purple stems of this weird, leafless, scaly-stemmed plant come poking up through the turf like miniature missiles.

Alderney is the only island in the Bailiwick to have moles. Folklore has it that St George, the patron saint of Guernsey, picked up all the moles and toads in that island, to rid the people of pests. He dropped some of the moles in Alderney and the others, along with the toads, in Jersey. Like the other Channel Islands, the European white-toothed shrew is found on Alderney, but not in the UK. Pipistrelle, long-eared and greater horseshore bats are found and other species may also occur.

SARK

Sark is a feudal society, and most things worth discovering about the island are governed by this one fact. The island's law, way of life and its popularity are all influenced by the system, and the great irony is that in the 20th century, a time capsule from a different era can be more successful than the most modern places in the world.

Sark lies nearly eight miles east of Guernsey. To reach the island the boat crosses the Little Russel to pass Jethou, and the Great Russel between Herm and Sark. The journey takes about 35 minutes by fast launch. The Isle of Sark Shipping Company operates a number of ferries and a cargo boat to the feudal island. It is cheaper to catch the first boat of the day to Sark, and possible to stay there until 7 p.m. You can hire a bike for the day, make a determined effort to walk right around the island, or enjoy the sun at Dixcart Bay, the only large beach available.

Sark is a plateau some 200ft above the sea, two miles long and surrounded by cliffs. To the south it is joined to Little Sark by an isthmus which is the same height but only 10 yards wide at the top. Little Sark is just under a mile long, but larger than Brecqhou, a separate island which lies at the base of Sark's west coast cliffs.

The roots of today's feudal society were put down by Queen Elizabeth I. In 1565 she granted Letters Patent to Helier de Carteret, a Jerseyman who colonised Sark. These are the basis of today's law, and were designed to protect the tenure and ownership of some 40 parcels of land, known as tenements. The owners had to supply a man each to form a militia, which defended the settlement. Each owner had a farmhouse, a piece of the excellent farmland, and a cotil or section of cliff grazing.

After an abortive attempt to form a court without royal authority, de Carteret's son Phillipe, who succeeded his father after the latter went back to Jersey, finally received permission to appoint a Seneschal (judge), Greffier (registrar), and Prevot (sheriff), still the leading figures in today's political assembly, the Chief Pleas. The 40 tenants and nine deputies, elected by the population of about 550, also sit in the assembly, which is held three times a year in the schoolroom close to St Peter's Church.

Since Phillipe de Carteret there have been 21 Seigneurs, of whom three have been women taking the title Dame of Sark. Mr. Michael Beaumont, the present Seigneur, is the grandson of the last of these women, Dame Sybil Hathaway.

SARK'S HARBOURS

Sark has two harbours within a few yards of each other: La Maseline, where the vast majority of visitors land, and the older Creux Harbour which was founded by the first Seigneur of Sark, Helier de Carteret, in 1588. For 23 years he and the other settlers had to make use of a landing at L'Eperquerie at the northern tip of the island, bringing all their worldly goods through this tortuous route. It was quite clear that an alternative had to be found, but Sark is surrounded by cliffs and the best site — the Baie de la Motte — was inaccessible. However, a good road could be made up the hill from Chaussee Chenchannee on the far side of the cliff above the bay and so a tunnel was driven through. The development which took place created Creux Harbour, said by many to be the most attractive haven in the Channel Islands.

Seigneur of the time, Rev. William Thomas Collings, had favoured the L'Eperquerie site, but once the Chief Pleas decided on improving the Creux he put himself wholeheartedly behind it, lending £3,200 towards the cost.

Rev. Collings had inherited the fief when his mother, Dame Marie, died a year after buying it for £6,000. She paid the balance of £1,400 after foreclosing on a mortgage, taken out around 1840, by the previous Seigneur, Ernest Le Pelley. He lost all his money mining silver on Sark, and his son, Peter Carey Le Pelley, could not keep up with the repayments on the loan and sold the fief in 1852. Dame Marie was the daughter of privateer Guernseyman Jean Allaire, widow of Thomas Guerin Collings, and great-great-grandmother of Dame Sybil Hathaway.

Maseline Harbour

Marie's fortune is said to have come from her father's outright piracy, but the money was finally put to good use as Rev. Collings invested it to develop Sark's tourist business. Besides the harbour improvement scheme, he built two hotels, the Dixcart, in its present position, and the Victoria which stood at the top of Harbour Hill on the site now occupied by the Bel Air. Collings blasted a hole through a cliff, forming the Window in the Rock. During the 1870s, Sark had between 4,000 and 5,000 visitors a year.

Landing was still a problem, however. Creux Harbour dried at low tide and the Sark fishermen used Les Laches as a mooring, only bringing in their boats up the slipway during bad weather. Discussions about an alternative landing started again in 1927, and by 1938 the decision had been taken to blast a tunnel through Pointe Cagnons, opposite the Creux entrance, into Maseline Bay. A jetty would run northwards and a bridge from the tunnel entrance would connect to the bottom of Harbour Hill. However, the bridge was smashed in a storm so the gully it crossed was filled. The stub of Maseline Jetty had been built when the Germans landed.

All work stopped until after the war when the jetty was completed. The price had risen, due to wartime inflation, from the £38,000 estimate, to £65,000. A loan was taken out to pay for the job and a poll tax imposed to repay the money. This was finally achieved in 1978, but the landing tax is still charged — it now goes into Sark's general revenue.

Creux Harbour

This lovely spot is often missed, partly because the tunnel leading to it is uninviting, sometimes because it is left for the return journey — time on Sark for the visitor is always short — but mostly because of the modern disease of rushing. Tractors pulling the aptly named toast-rack trailers which carry people to the top of Harbour Hill wait at the bottom to whisk visitors away before the area can be explored.

There were several attempts to build the breakwater at Creux, each washed away by storms, but in 1822 a jetty was built which lasted until 1866, when it was breached. The L'Eperquerie site, used centuries before by the early settlers, was again considered for a permanent harbour but the idea was rejected. Instead, £6,000 was spent on the Creux Harbour and a stronger breakwater was built. This had a quay on the inside of it, with the added luxury of landing steps, and a slipway for beaching fishing boats. A gap was left in the northern section of the harbour to allow surges of water, caused by large waves at high tide, to get out. This was not successful and has been filled in. The

THE VILLAGE

One of the advantages of exploring Creux and Maseline, before going up Harbour Hill, is that it gives time for the rush of people who get off the boat to disperse, before you set off for the village. The walk up to the top of the hill is steep, and for those who would rather, there is public transport available on the 'toast-rack', an adapted carriage pulled by a tractor. The walk up is pleasant, however, and a seat is placed half-way for the weary.

Close to the top of the hill, the road passes a barn which houses Sark's generating station. Its steady throb can be heard several yards away. Twenty yards further and the Bel Air is reached. There is a coffee bar, conveniences and a pub in the little complex of old and modern buildings. A little beyond it a line of horse-drawn carriages forms to offer the visitor a tour of the island. These passed, a crossroads is reached.

Ahead is The Avenue, a dusty street of ramshackle shops. Once an elegant tree-lined promenade, it is now fascinating in its disarray. It does bring to mind images of American ghost towns, although the spooks here do not get a look-in as French, English, Dutch and German visitors examine the goods for sale. Some say that The Avenue and village lack character but the area is of great interest. There is a post office, with Sark's only pillar box, two banks, and cafes.

Sark has little taxation; there is no VAT or purchase tax, just a small duty on tobacco and alcoholic drinks, making the village one of the cheapest places in the Bailiwick in which to shop. Visitors are liable to Customs' checks when they get back to Guernsey, but this does not seem to stop the shopping boom which takes place six days a week throughout the summer.

The road forks at the post office, the left road going to Le Manoir, a granite building which was the home of the Seigneur before La Seigneurie was built. Opposite is the junior school, and the two-celled prison building, still used today if Sark's cheap drink proves too heady. The right fork leads past the Greffe office to St Peter's Church, built in 1820 for £1,000. Many say the building is disagreeable and has little merit,

but it is well kept, homely and obviously loved by the Sarkese.

The road passes on to the Island Hall which is home to all sorts of local events. Usually overlooked, it is worth popping in — you may be surprised, as was the author who once found a meeting of Sark's women who offered tea, and pressed for news of Guernsey. The senior school is the last building in the street, and the crossroads at Clos a Jaon leads on to La Seigneurie, left along the route of the island tour, past the Methodist Chapel.

Turning right towards the east coast, along Rue du Sermon, a wide road leads down to the Carrefour crossroads. Straight through is a maze of lanes which lead to the hamlet of La Ville Roussel, and Point Robert Lighthouse. Left leads along Rue du Fort, which joins L'Eperquerie Road at the common. Turn right, and the Rue Lucas leads back to the top of Harbour Hill. It passes a narrow lane which leads to The Mermaid pub, home of darts, dances and social evenings.

Rue Lucas also passes the old Sark telephone building. In 1979 an automatic exchange was put in, replacing a dear telephonist who knew everything about everyone. Mrs Walsh would receive the call, coming via Guernsey, and the caller would ask for the number. The call might be put straight through, but often she would say that the Sark resident wanted was in the village, or with friends, and connect the caller to the shop or house being visited!

A modern pottery has been built on the left-hand side of Rue Lucas, some 75 yards from the top of Harbour Hill. Opposite is a cycle shop which hires out bikes, complete with maps and trouser clips, for a small sum. Be warned, however, — the roads are busy, and contrary to popular belief, far from traffic-free. There is one tractor for every seven people on Sark, about 50 horse-drawn vehicles, and swarms of cyclists, keeping to the left or right, depending on their country of origin. Tractors were first allowed for farming, then carting or general business use, and today they replace the car. Away from the village, however, cycling is fun, pleasant and relaxing.

LITTLE SARK

Little Sark is separated from the larger main island by a narrow isthmus called La Coupee, which is no joke to cross if you are scared of heights. It is 150 yards long, 260ft high and a mere 25ft across. In gale force winds nerves of steel must be needed as the air resounds with the shrieking of what sound like lost souls. It is the noise made by the wind as it whistles through the Cavern des Lamentes, at the base of Little Sark's eastern cliffs. Two people are said to have died after falling from La Coupee – Philippe Hamon was blown over while carrying corn to Dame Le Pelley in 1732, and Danny Lanahan, an Irish hotel worker, is said to have slipped while performing a handstand on the railing one dark night in 1975.

Railings protect the unwary, though, and no-one should be put off crossing into Little Sark. The main road leads to a village including La Sablonnerie Hotel, cafe and tea garden, a good place to rest, although the islet is less than a mile long it is quite a step from the top of Harbour Hill. The road forks, left to the old silver mines and the Venus Pool, and right to the Duval Farm and the five rock pools at Le Coursier.

The futile search for commercial quantities of copper, silver and lead resulted in ruin for the Le Pelley family who were Seigneurs from 1730 to 1852. Four shafts were dug, one under the sea bed, by 250 Cornish miners. By 1847 it was all over. More than £30,000 had been spent and Ernest Le Pelley, ruined and broken, died two years later. Little Sark has several mine shafts,

La Coupee

The silver mines

many overgrown, but not all useless. Waste disposal on Sark has always been a problem but the people of Little Sark dump their rubbish down Prince's mineshaft.

The path past the silver mines leads to Point a Clouet, overlooking the huge stack of L'Etac de Sercq, a thriving bird colony in the spring. It offers one of the best chances of seeing puffins, which bob on the surface of the sea in the coves around the cliff.

The road from La Sablonnerie, past Duval Farm, leads to a deep rock pool at Moie de la Bretagne. Less well known than the Venus Pool, but possibly better for swimming, the Adonis Pool is deeper, more irregularly shaped and longer. It is only accessible at low tide and there is more of a scramble to reach it — a journey for the sprightly, and not to be attempted alone.

A little further around the corner is another landing at Moie de la Fontaine, almost landlocked by the huge rock which shelters the spot. The swimming here is superb and you are watched over by a bust of Queen Victoria. At least, that is what one of the rocks close by is said to resemble. The cliffs above Vermandez and Grande Greve Bay have superb views of the arch in Point le Jeu and are a fitting backdrop as Little Sark is left via the Coupee.

LA SEIGNEURIE

The house is at the head of a valley, rising up from Port du Moulin, which carries one of the largest streams on the island. The gardens, open on Mondays and Wednesdays, give limited access to the outside of La Seigneurie, which is closed to the public. The gardens are well worth the small entrance fee charged. They are beautifully kept and, protected by a high wall from the terrible winter winds, contain a host of plants collected by the late Dame of Sark and Mr Michael Beaumont, the current Seigneur. A walk around the grounds, beside being of interest to gardeners, is also an excellent opportunity for birdwatchers to visit a pool at the head of the stream — a good place to watch migrant flycatchers and warblers.

The pond is said to have been made by monks as one of a series of carp 'stew ponds' which, beside supplying fresh fish, provided water power for Le Moulin, or mill, further down the valley. La Seigneurie was built on the site of an old monastery set up by St Magloire; the popular date for this event is AD 565, exactly 1,000 years before Sark was granted to Helier de Carteret by Elizabeth I, but the coincidence seems too good to be true. The monastery was a school for nobleman's children from the nearby coast of France. It was sacked by Norse raiders in the middle of the ninth century, leaving a pile of stones in the Seigneurie grounds and a wealth of folklore and stories.

La Seigneurie is the home of the Seigneur, and has been since 1730 when Susanne Le Pelley, the daughter of Jean Le Gros, bought the Fief of Sark. The house, which she already owned, was then called La Perronerie after the perron, a wide flight of stone steps leading to the front door. It replaced Le Manoir, which was given to the minister and was enjoyed by successive vicars until 1934 when it was sold. Susanne's acquisition of the fief had something of an ironic twist as the loosening of the Le Gros family's hold on Sark's property and government had been a major exercise for the de Carteret family who preceded them as Seigneurs.

A signalling tower stood in the grounds of the house so that the Collings family, who succeeded the Le Pelleys when silver mining failed in 1852, could keep in touch with Guernsey. They lived in Sark only in the summer and used the tower while in residence. It became useless after trees blocked the view, and a replacement, attached to the house, was built by Rev. William Collings. This is not a pleasant feature of La Seigneurie and his grand-daughter, the Dame of Sark, wanted to remove it, but the cost was too high.

The gardens are entered from Moinerie Road, through a pair of superb ornamental wrought-iron gates, given to Dame Sybil on her marriage to American - born Robert Hathaway in 1929. He became joint Seigneur and was a most popular man in the island. It was the second marriage of the Dame. Her first husband, Dudley Beaumont, died of Spanish 'flu, leaving her with six children to raise. They had married in London after 17-year-old Sybil Collings, as she was then, was thrown out of La Seigneurie when her father heard of the couple's wedding plans. Mrs Hathaway left Sark and worked with the British Army of Occupation in Germany, where she learned the language, little realising the importance it would hold for her. By then she and her father had reconciled their differences, and after he died in 1927, Dame Sybil Beaumont took her seat in the Chief Pleas.

After her marriage to Robert Hathaway, a naturalised Briton who had left the USA in protest at the prohibition laws, the couple set about stamping their mark on Sark while maintaining the way of life which has remained successful to this day. An artists' colony was set up, and the Island Hall was built to provide much needed recreation facilities. Construction of La Maseline jetty was started and La Seigneurie became the venue for many bridge parties.

This peaceful scene was shattered by the German Occupation, but La Dame managed to retain her home and exerted great influence on the island's new rulers. Even so she could not prevent deportation, along with two large Sark families, of her husband, who as a non-islander was interned in Germany. Despite gaining great popularity in Laufen Camp, his health was broken by the experience. He died in 1954 shortly after their silver wedding anniversary.

La Dame died on 14 July 1974. The position of Seigneur went to her grandson, Michael Beaumont, missing a generation for the first time, as his father had been killed during the war. Mr Beaumont was an aero-engineer in Bristol, and had to adjust to the complete contrast of his new life, but for his wife, Sark-born Diana La Trobe-Bateman, it was a homecoming. Much of the 12-bedroomed Seigneurie was in need of repair and Mr Beaumont became Sark's first feudal ruler to work for his living since Helier de Carteret.

Michael Beaumont inherited certain feudal rights when he became Seigneur. He alone is allowed to keep an unspayed bitch longer than 28 days, a length of time calculated to allow visitors to bring their pets with them. His permission for the sale of land, known as conge, has to be obtained before any such transaction, and by his right of treizieme he receives one thirteenth part of the the sale price of any property. The Seigneur is the only person allowed to keep pigeons, and an ornate dovecote, built in the grounds of La Seigneurie in 1730, is home to a flock of white fantails.

HORSE AND CART RIDES

Everyone must try a trip on a horse and cart just once in a lifetime, and Sark offers the ideal opportunity. There is something which makes this form of travel very exciting, and certainly a feeling of superiority is detected by people on foot as they are overtaken by passengers riding effortlessly, high above them. The four great advantages to this, the slowest form of 20th-century travel, are the peace, the excellent view, the commentary and the relaxation. Walking around Sark on a hot day can be tiring and riding in style is often preferable.

The commentary is probably the most important part of the journey. To get a good commentary, try to choose a cart driven by an old Sark resident, rather than one of the young, imported guides who go to the island for the summer. The youngsters are good — they have to take a driving test — but Sark cannot be in their blood as it is with the Sarkese.

There are five governess carts, five victorias, 24 vans and 22 wagonettes registered on the island, although the last two classes are the most usual kinds seen on the roads. They line up along the roadside at the top of Harbour Hill, their 'cabbies' touting for trade as people walk by.

Each vehicle is equipped with a set of steps which lead up through a tiny latch gate into the cart. Some have one or two places up with the driver who sits on a bench behind the horse. The horses are characters and receive a great deal of attention from passengers, particularly at the stopping places. They take it in turns to work and, like the humans behind them, get the occasional day off. Free in the fields, the resting horses call to their working companions as the carriages pass.

The route taken turns right at the top of the hill at La Collinette, following Rue Lucas out of the village to the Carrefour crossroads. Here, passing one of the many old houses which now has a corrugated iron roof instead of the original thatch, the vehicle sets off along Rue du Fort, towards L'Eperquerie Common. A path running down to the right leads to the home of the Channel Islands' finest ornithologist, Phillip Guille, who spends most of his life catching, ringing and releasing the many migrant birds which stop to drink and feed in the wet valley running through his property.

The trip continues round to the common where a stop is made on days when La Seigneurie gardens are closed. The view out across Le Platon takes in the islands of Brecqhou to the left, and Guernsey, Jethou and Herm in front, masking St Sampson's, and to the right Alderney. If the grounds are open, a stop is made at La Seigneurie, with time to look around the gardens. When it reaches the crossroads opposite Sark's school, the carriage turns right, along Rue du Sermon. Passing the Wesleyan Chapel, the road turns sharp left before running, in an almost straight line, down to La Coupee more than a mile away.

Here everyone piles out to gasp at the 260ft drop and look across to Little Sark. It is the farthest most visitors go; few walk over and explore Sark's small cousin. As we have seen, they are the losers. To the right is Grande Greve Bay, while in the distance, out beyond L'Etac rock, lies the island of Jersey. The nearest fief on that island, St Ouen, is the home to this day of the de Carteret family, whose ancestor Helier was the first settler and Seigneur on Sark. He built the wide, straight roads and, under the rule of his family, the hedges and banks were made to separate the 40 tenements.

The cart retraces its outward route along the undulating, dusty, Rue de la Coupee, passing a turning on the right to the cool, tree-filled valley leading down to Dixcart Bay. Further up the road back to the village, on the left, is Happy Valley with the hamlet of Dos d'Ane, which means donkey's back.

The cart turns right at La Vauroque into Rue du Moulin, leading back to Le Manoir. It passes the highest spot on Sark at the old mill, which was built by Helier de Carteret in 1571 and last milled corn in 1919 after being brought back into use in the First World War. Used as a lookout post by the Germans who, during the Occupation, made good use of its position 356ft above sea level, it has now been converted into a three-storey gift shop. The cart ends its journey by either looping past St Peter's Church, or carefully picking its way through the village to La Collenette, at the top of Harbour Hill.

HERM

Herm is as close to a romantic desert island as you will find in Europe — in fact the tenant, Major Peter Wood, said that if he could select a perfect island and place it anywhere in the world, Herm would be it and he would put it just off Guernsey.

The island is 1½ miles long by half a mile wide and tapers northwards with sheer cliffs to the south and beautiful white sand beaches around the north. It is topped by a farm which runs one of the biggest herds of Guernsey cows in the Bailiwick.

Three ferry companies ply the waters between St Peter Port and Herm. Some are old and slow, giving time for sightseeing on the journey and time to relax into a leisurely frame of mind. Other ferries, run by Trident Travel, are large, powerful and fast, often carrying tractors and cows, and always laden with supplies for the hotel and village community. They start their service early in the morning with the 'milk run', allowing day visitors up to 10 hours on the island.

On a good day more than 1,000 tourists visit Herm. The place never seems crowded however, as the main interest of most visitors is sunbathing and there are many beaches to select. There are other attractions — the fishing is terrific and naturalists often have a field-day watching birds, flowers and insects which abound in their seasons. The island is regarded as a playground for Guernsey people and many take their summer holidays there.

HERM HARBOUR

Seen from the sea as you arive after a 15-minute crossing from Guernsey, Herm's harbour gives a hint that something quite different is about to be experienced. Its arm, which juts out from the pleasantly wooded shopping area, is a bustle of activity. Luggage and provisions on board the boat are unloaded, and there is always a small queue of people waiting to make the crossing in the other direction. The harbour may have up to 20 visiting yachts and boats moored and there are usually a few small boys fishing from the quay. Tanks of heating oil, cylinders of butane gas, milk churns from Guernsey's Dairy and even the odd cow clutter the jetty. The boats never stop long and are quickly unloaded and made ready for their return.

Your voyage to Herm passes many small rocks, some of them just under the water, others marked to guide boatmen to and fro. Five are marked with letters corresponding to their names. The first to be seen is Creux. Alligande and Godfrey are next, and Epec and Vermerette are passed just before you reach Herm. All can be seen through binoculars from the harbour. Two obvious marks are on the hillside to the left of the Mermaid Tavern and are lit at night. The white iron structures stand about 10ft high, and when they appear one above the other as seen from the sea, they lead boats straight into the harbour mouth.

As you stand on the jetty, next to the old crane, face inland. In front of you is the main shopping area of Herm — two souvenir shops, a pub and restaurant are to the left and the White House Hotel is to the right. A few fishermen's cottages, now rented out as self-catering apartments, mark the start of the long hill up to Le Le Manoir village. Behind the jetty is one of the few signs of modern life — a yellow telephone box. To the left is Herm's administraion office — a flat roofed building which is home to a small colony of house martins whose cup-shaped nests can be seen under the eaves.

The crossroads behind the administration office will provide you with information about the island. There is a signpost telling how to get to the various places of interest and a notice board with the rules and regulations of Herm (no radios or tape recorders can be played, for example). As there are no cars allowed on the island all distances are measured in minutes — the time it takes to walk to your destination.

Although the shopping area looks pretty now, it has had a turbulent past. Developed around 1800 to service granite quarrying, it was a rough, industrial eyesore employing 400 men. The harbour had two arms and was built to load granite onto ships bound for England, where the stone was used to build railway bridges and tunnels during the Industrial Revolution.

Herm granite is of great hardness and density and was taken to the harbour piers along railway lines, the tracks of which can still be seen as you arrive. The second harbour arm ran out to Hermetier (known as Raz Island) from Fisherman's Beach to the north of the harbour. It has now been washed away, although a causeway can still be seen at low tide.

The island had its own prison, built to take drunken granite workers whose behaviour got out of hand. Gang warfare was rife during the short heyday of the granite industry and the gaol can still be seen. The bee-hive shaped lock-up marks the north-west corner of a tennis court in front of the hotel.

There were three quarries on the island but only traces of two can be seen today. The first, Monku Quarry, is up on the hill behind Fisherman's Cottage and will be seen as you head north to the Common and Shell Beach. La Chausee, the second quarry, is behind the hotel but cannot be seen as it is completely overgrown. The third, now used as a rubbish dump, is between the shops and Rosiere Steps, where you disembark from the ferries when the harbour dries out at low tide.

The area around the harbour is a mix of older granite cottages and modern properties built by Italian craftsmen who gave the shopping precinct a Mediterranean atmosphere. The two shops sell a range of gifts including Herm stamps, which are now no longer valid but have become collectors' items. The Mermaid pub and restaurant offer a range of light meals while the Ship, part of the White House Hotel, offers a good lunch.

A WALK AROUND HERM

This walk takes between two and three hours and goes around the island's coast, covering a distance of about four miles. It includes most of the bays, the common and south coast cliffs. On a hot day, refreshment stops at Shell Bay, Belvoir and the shopping centre will be welcome.

Belvoir Bay

Set off from the shopping centre northwards along the flat path which runs above Fisherman's Bay. You will notice that the vegetation to your left, running down the bank to the sand, is made up of tall reeds. These are *Phragmites* reeds, normally found in freshwater marshes and used elsewhere for thatching. Their presence along this salt-sprayed coast is explained by the escarpment to your right which runs down from Le Manoir. Rain falling on the hill is not channelled into a stream, but runs under the path to provide a freshwater habitat for the reeds, even at the edge of the sea.

The path continues past picturesque Fisherman's Cottage with Monku Hill and its quarry behind. Just past a wood consisting mostly of elms, the path emerges through a gateway on to the common. Before going through the gate, turn to your left and visit Herm's tiny cemetery, the burial place of two passengers who died of cholera on board a ship in 1832.

The ship's master had been refused entrance to St Peter Port because of the disease, so he diverted to Herm and paid quarry workers to bury the dead. They did so, carving a headstone from the soft Portland stone carried as ballast on the ship, but in the process they contracted the disease. It spread through the colony, killing 341 workers.

As you pass through the gate on to the common, there is another left turn which leads down to Bear's Beach. There, if you look back towards the harbour, a broad scree of rocks marks Monku Quarry and the remains of the northern jetty.

A broad path sets off across the common, which is dotted with rabbit scrapes and delicate lime-loving plants. After a few yards it reaches Robert's Cross, where several tracks meet between two hills — Le Petit Monceau on the left overlooking Bear's Beach and Le Grand Monceau standing to the right above Shell Bay. The site was marked by the earliest settlers on Herm with a tomb 16ft long and 7ft wide. It has suffered some disturbance, particularly by quarrying activities, but it is the best-preserved of Herm's Neolithic remains. Other graves can be found around the tops of the two hills. The Lukis family carried out several rescue digs on Herm and the finds are with Guernsey Museum.

Take the northern path to your left across the common, skirting Le Petit Monceau. It comes out at a charming little beach, Port es Vallais, which runs up to Oyster Point marking the north-west corner of the island.

Belvoir Bay

You can wander around the northern end of Herm either along Mouisonniere Beach, or above it on the sand dunes which make up the common. If you choose the latter, do not be tempted to go barefoot as the ground is covered with thousands of tiny burnet roses and the thorns will irritate for days. Halfway along the north coast you will reach an obelisk, put up to replace a large granite menhir called Longue Pierre which was shipped to London by quarry workers, angering local fishermen who used it as a navigation mark.

Alderney Point on the north-east corner of the island has dangerous currents running past it and swimming is banned for a hundred-yard stretch on either side. It marks the top end of Shell Beach — a long, white stretch of sand made up of small pieces of shell. Some of these fragments are said to have been carried in the Gulf Stream from as far away as the Gulf of Mexico.

The white shell sand reflects the rays of the sun, and make it a most popular beach for sunbathing. The swimming is good too, as the beach slopes steeply into the sea giving easy entrance into the water, particularly at high tide. After a swim you might fancy refreshments from the kiosk at the south end of the beach, before setting off along the coast path with Le Grand Monceau hill to your right.

Shell Beach

After a walk of about five minutes, the path goes round Fisherman's Point. Here you will get an excellent view of Belvoir Bay, which also has a beach kiosk to serve the many sunbathers and swimmers that congregate on its sands. A turning to the right goes up a little valley, past Belvoir House to Le Manoir.

Your coastal route continues, however, gently rising to a height of 100ft as it rounds the next headland to overlook Puffin Bay. You might, as the name suggests, be lucky enough to see the black and white puffins sitting on the water of the bay anywhere between here and the top of the cliffs at Barbara's Leap. At the end of July, the puffins leave for mid-Atlantic waters where they spend the winter.

The track rises more steeply now, rounding Moie Sercq headland with its view across the Great Russel channel to Sark and Brecqhou, and eventually reaching a great rift in the cliff at Barbara's Leap — at a height of about 150ft above sea level. The name recalls the adventure of a young woman who fell down the cliff here about 20 years ago, but suffered only cuts, bruises and shock! The gully is an ancient nesting site for ravens which may be seen robbing the gulls' nests during the summer.

The path dips down into a pretty, damp glade, headed by a stand of pine trees. This is Primrose Valley. It has a stream running down it which plunges (or rather trickles during the dry summer months) over a sheer cliff at Le Creux Pigeon. Deep in the undergrowth is a pipe and trough put in by Major Wood when he first came to the island and was searching for a water supply. A path runs off to your right up the valley, leading across the spine of Herm to Le Manoir village.

After rising out of Primrose Valley the coast path drops down Orr Steps coming round the south-west corner of Herm at Point Sauzebourge giving a superb view of Jethou with Guernsey behind it. Jethou was cut off from Herm by a terrible storm in AD 709 according to folklore. It has two islets — Grande Fauconniere to the south and Crevichon to the north. Both have large colonies of breeding gulls and shags, while Crevichon has a few puffins which nest in rabbit burrows along the top of a raised beach, on the shore facing Herm.

Sauzebourge Point is a good place to sit and get your breath back after the cliff walk. The path then continues northwards past an old mineral mine shaft before dropping down a flight of steps to the landing place at Rosiere. Another ten minutes walk will see you back at the harbour.

A final reminder of the quarrying industry can be seen from the path, however. Look out at Crevichon and you will notice that the conical island has been half quarried away leaving it looking like a cake with several slices missing. Mentioned in accounts for Castle Cornet in 1564 as having supplied stone for the building, it was bought by the States of Guernsey, together with Jethou, in the second half of the 19th century to secure a supply of stone for the new harbour of St Peter Port. It is said that the job of loading barges with stone at Crevichon, and sailing them to the construction site, was easier than getting granite from Guernsey quarries and hauling it by cart to the harbour.

LE MANOIR VILLAGE

On returning to The Drive turn right to pass a quaint row of fishermen's cottages and the island's power plant. A red water tender marked 'Herm Fire Brigade' is usually parked outside. The noise from the power station's three water-cooled, three-phase diesel generators is loud, but it does not deter swallows nesting in the barn next to it.

Ten families live and work on Herm all year round and Le Manoir is the focal point of their activities. The buildings include the island's power station, the carpenter's shop, the school, St Tugal's chapel and the home of Major and Mrs Wood. Le Manoir used to be the main farmstead but a new dairy farm was built in 1974, a short walk away between granite walls and pine trees to the south.

Le Manoir village is reached from the shopping centre by taking the steep path, called The Drive, towards Belvoir Bay. It winds through woods to the summit of the hill where it levels out between two stone walls. The one on your left protects what used to be a walled garden but is now used to graze young cattle and a few goats. The right-hand wall runs around the garden and field of Lady Perry's House — home of the Wood family since 1949.

St Tugal's Chapel, at the end of the wall, is more than 900 years old, founded by one of several monastic orders which have settled in Herm. It is used for services every Sunday morning — taken by Major Wood, usually with a guest organist recruited from among the residents.

The power plant stands at the junction of four paths. Turn right towards the south coast and the track passes a shelter built on to the side of a cottage called La Forge. It was here that the oxen used as draught animals were shod, but because, unlike horses, they cannot stand on three legs for long, the beasts had to be supported by belly straps while the shoeing was done.

The stamp of Prince Blucher, a descendant of the Prussian general at the Battle of Waterloo and tenant of Herm until 1914, is most noticeable in the next part of Le Manoir. It was he who built the keep, complete with battlements, visible to your right. He also planted the pine trees, some of which are now more than 100 years old, and converted the island's windmill into the round tower look-out post, also complete with battlements.

The lane leads on to the flat modern farm buildings from where more than 200 gallons of milk are daily transported, via the harbour, on the first boat to Guernsey Dairy. The herd of 120 cows produces three per cent of Guernsey's milk, some of which is then shipped back for consumption on Herm.

INDEX